MW00617986

Barbara
May God richly bless you!
Jason Frenn

BECOME WHAT YOU BELIEVE

The 10 Essential Characteristics of
Those Who Experience Miracles Today

Also by Jason Frenn

Power To Change
Breaking the Barriers
Power To Reinvent Yourself
The Seven Prayers God Always Answers

Become What You Believe

The 10 Essential Characteristics of
Those Who Experience Miracles Today

Jason Frenn

Summit Books, LLC
Jackson, Wyoming

Summit Books, LLC.

ISBN 978-0-9913881-0-3

Cover design Rick Cortez

Printed in the United States of America
First Edition: January 2014

Dedicated to

Two great people of faith
Two loving and caring Christians
Two pioneers of the work in Latin America
The two finest in-laws a son-in-law could ask for

Richard and Janice Larson

Contents

INTRODUCTION

As I stepped onto the stage the first night of the crusade in Barranca, Costa Rica, I was overwhelmed with compassion for the crowd of four thousand people who were living in a marginalized community. The Apostle Matthew's words came to mind describing Jesus' heart for those who suffer: "When he saw the crowds, he had compassion on them, because they were harassed and helpless, like sheep without a shepherd" (Matt. 9:36). Living in poverty and sickness takes a tremendous toll and makes people feel helpless. The people of Barranca had endured great struggle, pain, and sickness. As I was finishing the altar call of the crusade, suddenly an elderly woman and a teenage girl got around the security lines. They somehow sneaked past the guards, jumped over the barricades, and avoided the ushers next to the stage. They approached me rather aggressively, but since they didn't seem to be armed, I wasn't too alarmed.

The elderly woman, who identified herself as Victoria, said, "Brother Jason, the last time you held a crusade in this city was in 2003. I spoke to you the last night of that crusade. Do you remember me?"

I said, "No, I'm very sorry. That was nine years ago."

By now, the guards were approaching, and the ushers surrounded us. I gestured to the security team to hold off and asked Victoria to keep talking.

She said, "At the time, my three-year-old granddaughter, Stephanie, was unable to walk. Her back and hips were out of alignment, and the doctors at the clinic did not have the necessary means to operate. With a sense of great desperation, we brought her to the crusade the final night believing God for a miracle. I distinctly remember walking into the big white tent that held five thousand people. The service was already over, and people were leaving. Half the lights were turned off, and you were standing at the foot of the stage. My husband carried our granddaughter over to you in his arms, and we asked if you would pray for her. After we explained the entire story, you asked only one question, 'Do you believe God can do this?'"

As Victoria told me the story, tears began flowing down her cheeks. She covered her mouth—her hand slightly shaking—and after a few seconds, she regained her composure. She continued, "I said, Absolutely! You prayed with us, and since that night, for nine years, I've wanted to tell you that God healed my granddaughter of that paralyzing condition. We began to see improvement as soon as we got home, and within three days, she was completely healed."

Victoria finished by saying, "Today, she is in perfect health and has been ever since that night. Brother Jason, this is my granddaughter, Stephanie." Standing next to her was the young teenager. I embraced both of them and thanked the Lord for the powerful miracle. Once again, I was overwhelmed, but this time with gratitude for God's mercy. I glanced over, and the ushers were wiping tears from their eyes too. One of the guards turned to the other and said, "I need to start going to church again."

As missionary evangelists who hold evangelistic outreaches in public places such as plazas, parks, stadiums, and major intersections, my wife and I have seen countless miracles. We've seen thousands of people delivered from demonic oppression. In over 160 nights of open-air outreaches in the tropics, we've only had to cancel two nights on account of rain. We have ministered in half the countries of Latin America, mostly in places where poverty is great and delinquency is high. It is in those areas, however, that God's miracle-working power is evident. The Bible says, "He will take pity on the weak and the needy and save the needy from death. He will rescue them from oppression and violence, for precious is their blood in his sight" (Ps. 72:13–14).

Throughout my travels, I have noticed a greater frequency of the miraculous in places outside Western Europe and North America, especially where there is great need. Why is that? Is there something about those two continents that impedes God's miracles and revival? This book aims to answer that question.

The answer, in part, involves whether we believe (or refuse to believe) in the supernatural. People who embrace an anti-supernatural worldview rarely experience miracles, and even if they did experience the miraculous, they probably wouldn't recognize it as such. Those who refuse to believe in a God who interacts with his creation rarely experience spiritual breakthroughs. They rarely experience healing, deliverance, and most importantly, they will never experience salvation. At the core of the sin of blasphemy is a refusal to believe in a God who performs miracles.

As the Old Testament records, the Israelites witnessed ten unparalleled plagues. God split the Red Sea in two so they could cross to the other side on dry ground. They watched as drinking water flowed from a rock. God provided dew in a desert for forty years so they could eat manna every day. Their shoes never wore out, and they never went hungry. Yet in the midst of God's miraculous provision, the writer of the book of Hebrews clearly states that an entire generation died in the desert because of their *unbelief* (Heb. 3:19). How is that possible? It is almost inconceivable.

Three thousand three hundred years later, we are not far behind the wandering Israelites, struggling with our own unbelief. The same spiritual sickness that kept them in a holding pattern for forty years continues to plague us today. It spreads like a cancer across the continents of the world.

The Biggest Challenge in the Last One Hundred Years

As a missionary, my heart aches for those who have no food or shelter. I am deeply concerned for those who cannot afford proper medical care and even more for those who do not live where it's available. Poverty, racism, sexism, and bigotry are all significant problems that the church has faced over two millennia. It can be argued that we've made significant advances in these areas in the last century. However, there is a greater challenge that the church faces today. In North America and Western Europe, New Testament faith among the general populace has been dwindling over the past one hundred years. Fewer people attend church across most denominations as a percentage of the total population, and there are fewer church services each week per capita.[1] Many people question the existence of God, and if he does exist, they wonder if he interacts with humans as the Bible stories indicate.

Convincing people to place their faith in God is a greater challenge than solving the world's poverty, sickness, and war. The secularized paradigm and the distinct separation between the natural and the supernatural have all but destroyed our faith in God. If we lose this battle, every other battle may be lost as well! Faith in God is the most essential value we have as believers. Without it, we'll be thrust into *saeculum obscurum* (the dark ages) once again.

The Number One Question

As a missionary to Latin America, I am asked by Christians in North America one question more than any other: "Why don't we experience the miracles that happen in other parts of the world?" Is it because God doesn't love us or that he favors other people more? Could it be that he is phasing out miracles because of all the advances in technology and modern medicine? Might it be because God doesn't care about those who suffer? None of these responses is true. God never turns his back on those who call upon his name.

Throughout the pages of this book, I will answer the question of why we don't see miracles like those who live in other areas of the world. The ten reasons I outline might surprise you. More importantly, though, is the question, can we do anything about it? The answer is an unequivocal *yes!* I will lay out in each chapter several important steps we can take to reverse this trend so that we can experience the miraculous with greater frequency.

Before we embark upon this important journey to rediscover what I call *New Testament faith*, we need to keep in mind several important pillars of truth. First, those who experience the miraculous, especially those who live in different areas of Asia, Latin America, and Africa, have a different paradigm for understanding the world than we do. They are wired differently than we are. Simply put, their worldview is like a puzzle, and God, aside from family, is by far the largest piece. In our puzzle, by contrast, we have reduced God to a small, almost insignificant piece. If we are going to experience the miraculous, then we must make God a much larger piece of our puzzle and at the same time reduce the complexities that distract us from living a life mindful of the spiritual world around us.

Second, people in the Bible, as well as those living in other parts of the world, are just like you and me. Now you're probably saying, "Wait, didn't you just say that we're different?" Yes. But we are all similar in many ways. We all have the same worries, challenges, and setbacks. We also have the same desires, aspirations, hopes, dreams, and victories. How can I say that? Well, as one of my mentors Zig Ziglar said on many occasions, "*Everyone* wants to be happy, healthy, and reasonably prosperous. We all want healthy family relationships, decent friendships, peace of mind, and hope for the future."[2] These are absolutes found in every culture. These are universal and timeless aspirations. From this perspective the differences between us are small. Our desires and challenges are relative. They depend upon where we live, the size of the challenge, and at which stage we are in life.

Third, while it may be difficult to not overanalyze every concept, try and hear what I am saying in the spirit I am saying it. It is my profound desire to help you see God's hand working in your life. I know that at some point you will need a miracle or perhaps many. However, seeing God's hand will be impossible if you limit yourself to picking apart the ten characteristics that are real and active in the lives of those who experience the power of God firsthand. The only way to experience that same power is to become humble like them, and open your heart to what God truly desires to do. For many of us, the more educated we are, the more difficult it is to turn off the filters that critique, discount, and eventually belittle the walk of faith. There is a good reason not one of the Pharisees, Sadducees, or Scribes ever received a miracle. Their mindset was dogmatic, condescending, and arrogant. They felt that they knew it all. So our mindset must be sincere but never critical, arrogant, presumptuous, or prideful.

Finally, we must remember that of the several theological foundations in Jesus' ministry, faith is the one he stresses as absolutely essential to cast out demons, heal the sick, and preach to the spiritually lost. This book deals with God's love. It deals with hope. But more than anything, this book deals with the first level of New Testament living—faith. Try and see faith as a language or a skill that we develop in our communication with God. The word *faith* is mentioned thirteen times in the Old Testament but over two hundred times in the New Testament. Jesus strongly urges his followers to have and develop this core language, because without it we cannot adequately communicate with him.

This is precisely why I believe that, depending upon where you are in life, this book could be one of the most important books you read aside from the Bible. How can I say that? Faith is the foundation upon which we build our relationship with God. It is the most central focus of teaching in Christ's ministry. Without it, it is impossible to please God (Heb. 11:6). Yet there are few biblical communicators who understand what faith is, and those who do understand it, find it difficult to explain it to others. Jesus lost his patience on numerous occasions with his disciples because they just couldn't *get it*. My goal is to explain New Testament faith so that you can apply it to your everyday life and live it.

When you read the stories, absorb the teachings, and grasp the insights of those whose eyes have seen the miraculous, I pray you hear the Lord's voice, as if he himself were talking to you. I am not interested in convincing you with my words; instead, it is my desire that the Lord speak directly to your heart.

The Road Map

One of the challenges I faced in writing this book about faith was to keep it from being too academic. After all, faith cannot be quantified or broken down in a lab, which is what Western society trains us to do. I discovered that many times a Western mentality is opposed to faith. There is a bias against the supernatural. For this reason, I've looked at what some scholars are writing about the topic, but I especially focus on the commonalities of those who experience miracles, including New Testament believers and modern-day followers of Christ. As I mentioned earlier, people who live where miracles are prevalent have a different mindset than Westerners. I felt it would be best to try to write this book from their perspective. I interviewed hundreds of people who experienced miracles and asked them what they believe and why. I spent many hours praying and asking God to direct my efforts so that you can have something life-changing in your hands.

Even though it is challenging to find empirical evidence to support the idea that miracles are more frequent overseas than they are in the United States and Western Europe, there are consistent and legitimate observations that support this notion. Virtually every missionary who has lived extensively overseas shares this conviction. Even expatriates make similar observations about faith and church life overseas in comparison to Western Europe and North America. An overwhelming amount of observation outweighs the fact that few formal studies have been done.

In writing this book, I sought the input of one of the great authorities on this topic, Dr. Craig S. Keener, a professor at Asbury University. His exhaustive book on miracles, *Miracles:*

The Credibility of the New Testament Accounts, articulates the premise that antisupernaturalism has diluted faith in Western civilization. His findings give strong weight to the central focus of this book, and show why my observations indicate that there are fewer miracles here than in other parts of the world.[3] Dr. Keener has researched miracles, documented supernatural occurrences around the world, and most importantly, understands the crucial juncture at which we find ourselves.

For far too long we've talked about things, theorized our reality, hypothesized our experiences, and done little more than philosophize when it comes to experiencing the miraculous. By nature, that is the way Westerners are. As a result, miracles are infrequent in Western Europe and North America. I am convinced that if we do not experience miracles in our lives, we need to be re-discipled by those who are humble, who have faith the size of a mustard seed, and then practice what the Lord instructs us to do in his Word.

This book provides a clear understanding of where we stand today in relationship to those who walked with Christ and experienced his power. It answers some of the most difficult questions we face regarding faith, miracles, revival, and spiritual awakening. It will help us acquire a holistic view of God's creation as well as nine other characteristics found in those who experience the miraculous. Each chapter shows the similarities between the worldview of our friends in other parts of the world and those who experienced miracles in the New Testament.

We will also learn several practical things that we can do to alter the course of unbelief and take on a New Testament paradigm. At the conclusion of each chapter, I've included a prayer as a model for you. It's a prayer that asks God to help us to put into practice what we learn in each chapter. Feel free to say the prayers aloud. In the days and weeks following, be sure to write down God's response to your prayers.

Some say that miracles happen all around us all the time, even in the United States and Western Europe; we simply need the eyes to see them. I believe this is true. However, more than twelve times in the four Gospels, Jesus referred to people's faith as the reason for their miracle. On several occasions, he went on to say, "I have not seen such great faith." This strongly suggests that people possess something that moves the hand of God. The essence of New Testament faith is what this book is about.

Recently, I heard my father-in-law, Richard Larson, share a story found in Matthew 9:27–31. It's about two blind men who followed Jesus from one place to another screaming at the top of their lungs, "Mercy, Son of David! Mercy on us!" There is no indication in the story that Jesus acknowledged the two men during his journey home, but when he arrived, they walked in uninvited. The Lord turns to them and says, "Do you really believe I can do this?" They say, "Why, yes, Master!" Most translations say, "According to your faith will it be done to you." But the version my father-in-law read from, The Message, says, "He touched their eyes and said, 'Become what you believe.' It happened. They saw." When I heard him read those words, I knew that I needed to write this book and call it *Become What You Believe*. You see, our faith determines who and what we become. Inevitably, we become what we believe. So I pray that your faith be profoundly inspired as a result of what you encounter in these pages. May you experience phenomenal miracles, and above all, may you *become what you believe!*

Chapter One
PARADIGMS AND MIRACLES

I sat across the table from Tom, in utter amazement. He was one of the smartest students I knew but he couldn't recall the significance of one of the simplest parables. Five years earlier, he had explained it to me with ease. I said, "Tom, don't you remember the significance of the Parable of the Sower?" He replied, "This all sounds a bit familiar, but to be honest, I'm having a hard time seeing what you mean."

Tom was intelligent, read constantly, and was always at the top of his class. He eventually graduated and went on to build a successful career. Something changed after his first two years in Bible college, though. He began to question the legitimacy of his faith. After graduating, he gravitated toward another belief system that says, "Seeing is believing, and if I can't see it, I don't believe it." Eventually, his zealous faith in Christ diminished to cultural Christianity, which declined to agnosticism and finally atheism. "How could higher education damage one's walk of faith?" I wondered. Unfortunately, Tom is not alone. Millions of people in Western civilization are affected by a worldview that tells them that truth is discovered only by gathering evidence. Because the supernatural is impossible to quantify, we cannot prove its authenticity. Therefore, it doesn't exist.

Recently, I had an eye-opening conversation with a dear friend concerning the fading of New Testament faith in our society. Joe Class has traveled the world and interviewed hundreds of people who have been persecuted for the cause of Christ. He has documented many miracles. During the course of our conversation, he shared a profound insight: If Satan were to plant a seed that would germinate over the centuries, slowly deteriorating and eradicating the principles of faith from society, he would have planted that seed during a pinnacle moment in a prominent place at the culmination of that culture's international influence. He would have chosen someone who was highly respected and influential. That person, according to my friend, was born in 384 BC. His name was Aristotle, a student of Plato.

Plato believed that creation was comprised of two worlds. The first one was a perfect world, spiritual and without flaws. The second world was a poor reflection of the perfect one. He called it the world of shadows. Plato believed that you and I live in this imperfect world. Aristotle, on the other hand, was much more scientific. He believed that we discover the truth by collecting empirical evidence. He argued that there was a separation between the natural and supernatural, and argued that Plato's understanding of creation was archaic and not provable. In essence, Aristotle believed that *seeing is believing*. He believed that if God existed, by definition he couldn't interact with the physical world, because by doing so he would lose his divinity.

Over the centuries, Aristotle's teaching prevailed. It spread throughout Europe, came across the Atlantic Ocean, and embedded itself in North American culture. We find Aristotelian philosophy and ways of thinking permanently engraved into who we are as Westerners.

Today, we have separation of church and state. Schools no longer allow prayer. Courtrooms no longer use the Bible for taking the oath to tell the truth. If one word could describe our paradigm, it would be *fragmented*.

We separate and compartmentalize nearly every area of our

lives. We have thousands of channels on cable TV for different interests and areas of life. We separate cooking programs from political ones and religious programs from educational ones. Even our church life has become increasingly segmented. When a family goes to church, there is a class or activity for every age group. Everything has a place in our complex world and nothing spills over or meshes with the other. And God? Well, we fit him into an hour-and-fifteen-minute segment on Sunday morning, that is, if there is not shopping to do or a playoff game to watch.

Christians in Latin America, Africa, and Asia have not followed the Aristotelian way of thinking. They believe God goes with them everywhere. Church is a family event. Their lives are not nearly as fragmented as ours, and there is hardly a separation between the natural and supernatural.

The Natural and Supernatural Coexist on the Same Continuum

As we begin our journey to discover New Testament faith, the first characteristic found in those who experience the miraculous is that they *see life as holistic*. This is as true for those who lived two thousand years ago as it is for those who live where miracles are prevalent today. Their paradigm has hardly changed. They don't fragment or compartmentalize their worlds. Family is a part of their career. They attend church together. Their homes are relatively close to their places of work. Their religious views are intertwined with their daily lives and profoundly affect the way they live. Those who experience miracles have a spirituality that doesn't shut down when they go to the market or when they deal with the authorities. In their minds, the natural and supernatural are part of one continuum where everything is connected. Activities in the supernatural realm create repercussions in the natural world and vice versa. They don't simply believe in God, the supernatural, angels, and demons; they see all of these forces interacting in every part of life in the natural world. The supernatural and natural worlds are intertwined and inseparable.

In the minds of those who experience miracles, it is impossible to *check Jesus at the door* when they enter their place of work. The notion of separation of church and state is ridiculous. How can you keep God out of a courtroom? How can you prevent demons from influencing secular minds? Is there such a thing as a school system free from religious influence? Absolutely not! Secularism, they would argue, is a religion. And like all religions, it is influenced by the supernatural.

Many of the massacres that take place in society—school shootings, terrorist attacks on innocent civilians, human trafficking, senseless acts of violence—may or may not be the result of mental illness. One thing is certain, though, those who embrace a holistic worldview see a collision between the natural and supernatural in such horrific actions. These atrocities are Satanic in nature. Those who see the natural and supernatural on one continuum argue that spiritual forces are behind these terrible occurrences.

Those of us who live in Western Europe and North America, on the other hand, have no problem flipping a switch and turning off our spirituality when we enter our place of work, stand in line at the bank, or shop at Wal-Mart. Then we can become spiritually minded again when we pull into the parking lot of our place of worship. We separate and fragment our worlds easily.

In addition, we look for ways to explain supernatural phenomena using sociological terms. That is why over the last half century, society began to reinterpret evil behavior simply as mental illness. Ministers are no longer asked to testify in a court of law whether or not someone is demon possessed. Rather, we consult psychiatrists or those who have studied the sciences. That people who engage in horrific behavior might be demon possessed is not considered a possible explanation. No, we've become a secular society with a worldview that is entirely material, concrete, and elemental. Let me add that many theologians in recent years have moved from describing revival in spiritual terms to explaining revival in sociological ones. They see revivals as movements of people groups and trends of the masses, but fail to make the connection between social transformation and what the Spirit of God is doing.

Don't misunderstand the heart of what I am saying. I am not saying there is a demon under every rock. I am not saying that there is a spiritual reason behind every tragedy. Nor am I suggesting that mental illness is not the reason people commit horrific acts of violence. I am simply saying that if we want to experience the miraculous, we need to become aware of the supernatural world around us and understand how it impacts our everyday lives. Otherwise, we will see God-orchestrated revival as simply a large social movement made up of people impacted through brilliant marketing. We will begin to see people who God delivered from addiction as fortunate individuals who tapped into their mental power of self-control. And instead of seeing God's healing someone of cancer, we'll simply think that the body's natural cancer-cell fighting capability is the sole reason for remission of the disease.

If you were raised in Western civilization, your worldview is biased against a life of faith. Whether you like it or not, you've been profoundly impacted by a philosophy that ignores the supernatural as a part of life. Satan doesn't exist. Evil doesn't either. People are not evil, nor do they engage in evil acts influenced by supernatural forces. Rather, this philosophy declares that the decisions we make and the consequences of our actions are nothing more than the result of chemical reactions in our brains. The supernatural is nothing more than hocus-pocus. As the saying goes, "I don't believe in God. I believe in science." This is the essence of Western philosophy, a fragmented worldview that seeks to understand the world through empirical evidence only. After all, seeing is believing.

The way we think, process, and make decisions is determined by the lens through which we see the world. We can debate, collect evidence, and dissect theories and formulas. We might even be able to explain the Parable of the Sower in logical terms, but can we explain it with spiritual understanding? Can we see the supernatural world with supernatural eyes? The Apostle Paul warns us about seeing the world through physical, natural lenses only.

Paul was educated by one of the most noted rabbis in history, Gamaliel. In Jerusalem, Paul had broad exposure to classical literature, philosophy, and ethics. In spite of his high level of education, he urges us, "Finally, be strong in the Lord and in his mighty power. Put on the full armor of God so that you can take your stand against the devil's schemes. For we are not fighting against flesh-and-blood enemies, but against evil rulers and authorities of the unseen world, against mighty powers in this dark world, and against evil spirits in the heavenly places" (Eph. 6:10–12, NLT-SE). He also asserts, "The weapons we fight with are not the weapons of the world. On the contrary, they have divine power to demolish strongholds. We demolish arguments and every pretension that sets itself up against the knowledge of God, and we take captive every thought to make it obedient to Christ" (2 Cor. 10:4–5). Friend, you and I are in a battle for the survival of New Testament faith during the twenty-first century in Western civilization, and unfortunately, we are losing the battle. Until we can embrace New Testament faith, we will hardly experience revival or miracles in our lands.

What Is the Essence of New Testament Faith?

New Testament faith can be seen in the way a child puts his trust in his father when contemplating the first leap into a swimming pool. The boy somberly stares at his father, who stands waist deep and patiently encourages the young lad to take the plunge. His daddy says, "Jump! I'll catch you." Any doubt is dwarfed by the child's deepest conviction that his father is more than capable of keeping him safe. Similarly, New Testament faith is believing God and taking him at his word. Christians in Latin America, Asia, and Africa trust God and believe that the Lord will do what he says he will do. They believe God interacts with creation today just as much as he did two thousand years ago. They also believe that they are directly connected to the first-century church that began in the Book of Acts. To them, these are not spiritual assumptions. They are facts. In the same way that Westerners believe in the laws that govern physics, people of faith believe in spiritual laws. To them, *believing is seeing*. These spiritual laws are based upon their trust in the Lord, much as a child trusts his or her parents.

In Mark 10 we find a wonderful story of how Jesus views the worldview of children. When the disciples rebuked the parents for bringing their children to Jesus to have him bless them,

Jesus was indignant. He said, "Let the little children come to me, and do not hinder them, for the kingdom of God belongs to such as these. I tell you the truth, anyone who will not receive the kingdom of God like a little child will never enter it" (Mark 10:14–15). Then after Jesus blessed them, a man approached him. This is where Mark draws a stark contrast between those who have the gift of faith and those who do not. "Good teacher," the man asked, "what must I do to inherit eternal life?" (v.17). Then after listing the commandments he should keep, the Lord dropped a bomb that decimated the man's understanding of salvation. "Go, sell everything you have and give to the poor, and you will have treasure in heaven. Then come, follow me" (v. 21). The man was devastated, because he had great wealth.

Then something interesting happens in the story. Jesus turns to his disciples and says, "How hard is it to enter the kingdom of God!" (v. 23). When they have no response, he directs his statement at those who have the faith to enter the kingdom of God. "Children, how hard it is to enter the kingdom of God!" (v. 24). He then goes on to say, "It is easier for a camel to go through the eye of a needle than for a rich man to enter the kingdom of God" (v. 25). The disciples are perplexed and ask each other, "Who then can be saved?" (v. 26). The answer isn't easy, especially for the educated, wealthy, and those who are entrenched in their adult thinking. Jesus looks at them and says, "With man this is impossible, but not with God; all things are possible with God" (v. 27). If you want New Testament faith, you must learn to trust God much like a child trusts a parent.

Several years ago, I was overwhelmed with the stress of having to raise a quarter of a million dollars for a crusade. The deadline was fast approaching, and I saw no possible way to reach the financial goal before the event. I walked into my oldest daughter's room to tuck her into bed that evening. She innocently asked, "Dad, is something wrong?" Celina was perceptive for a nine year old. As I sat down on the side of her bed, I paused for a brief moment and said, "Well, sweetie, it's complicated. I have to raise a bunch of money in less than a month. I really don't see how it will all come together." Then I cracked a smile in an attempt to not paint a bleak picture and said, "Daddy just needs a miracle." Suddenly her whole face lit up as she smiled and said, "Oh, don't worry, Daddy. God will give you what you need, because he loves you."

The faith of a child is amazing. In the end, she was right. Indeed, God provided everything we needed for the crusade. As a matter of fact, we ended up with five hundred extra dollars in our crusade account. For some reason, Celina had no doubt, but unfortunately I did. She saw something that I didn't. Or perhaps she saw something that I couldn't or wouldn't.

It's true, the older we get, the less trusting we become. We read the stories of people who make terrible mistakes, and those mistakes have a devastating affect on our ability to trust politicians, preachers, and people of influence. Even family members and those close to us can cast shadows on our confidence in others. This wears down our faith, and over time, we struggle to be people who see the good, who believe God for the miraculous and impossible. "Oh sure," we think, "good fortune comes to others, but will it come to me?" All in all, we must recognize that we are in a battle for New Testament faith. We must become guardians of every thought, as Paul said.

Three Principles for Developing New Testament Faith in a Material World

To those of us who struggle to see the supernatural world around us, God has given us a wonderful gift. We live in a time when advances in technology, travel, and communication have made the world a smaller place. This allows us to have more intimate contact with those who have a similar worldview to those who lived in the New Testament. This is one of the ways God is re-establishing faith around the globe. The following three principles will help bring you closer to a New Testament faith.

1. Always make God your starting point.

As we look at the different regions where God continues to perform miracles, healings, and revival, these people groups have that same holistic paradigm we see in the New Testament. In Mexico, for example, a non-Christian parent might take his sick child to a witch doctor before taking him to the medical doctor. Why? The superstitious parent sees the supernatural and natural worlds impacting each other. But Christians will ask their pastor, family, and friends to pray before they take their child to the doctor. Their first impulse is to seek God's redemptive hand. They believe that the Lord might use a doctor, a lawyer, a pastor, or some other person. Or he may miraculously resolve the issue. Regardless of the outcome or whom God uses, they see him as their source for everything. He is their provider. He is their protector. He is their healer. He is their redeemer and deliverer. Their spiritual eyes see the supernatural world.

2. Close the two-thousand-year gap.

We have a unique opportunity to learn from miracle-believing people groups. We can travel and get a sense of their context. When we do, their influence begins to rub off on us. Any time we leave our own context to visit another culture, a part of our paradigm is reshaped. Thus, if you want to experience a phenomenal breakthrough in your walk with Christ, get out of your daily routine. Get out of your comfort zone and spend time around those who have great faith.

In my book *Breaking the Barriers,*[1] I mention that we become the common denominator of the six people with whom we spend the most time. This is especially true when it comes to becoming someone of faith. So reach out to those who have humility and faith and who resemble true disciples of Christ. Yes, there may be a language barrier. Yes, there may be a significant geographical distance. But we can communicate via translators, computer programs, Skype, e-mail, and FaceTime, as well as periodic mission trips. The goal is to understand that we don't necessarily have something to teach them, but rather, they can teach us childlike faith to see the spiritual world like they see it. Your goal is to develop the same gift of faith they have. Push aside all of your tendencies to explain things away logically or rationalize the outcome of something inexplicable and see what the Bible calls the faith of a child. In doing this, you will get a glimpse of the faith of the New Testament two thousand years ago.

3. Remember, God created faith and logic.

Being logical and spiritual are not mutually exclusive. Paul was highly logical and spiritual at the same time. He did not sacrifice one for the other. This is true where miracles are prevalent around the world today. Believers in Latin America, Africa, and Asia are logical and operate and function like people in any culture. They are educated and show up to work to perform their duties. It could be argued that they perform their duties more effectively because they do not have the resources available to those who live in places like Western Europe and North America. They do not, however, sacrifice their spiritual eyesight as a result of living in a secular world. Their worldview helps them see the natural and supernatural at the same time, and they do not separate the two. This is a valuable lesson for all of us who desire to have New Testament faith.

If you want to experience the same miracles that are seen around the world, aim to bring faith and spiritual eyesight alongside your attention to logical detail. When Paul said, "We live by faith, not by sight" (2 Cor. 5:7), he echoed what our Lord said about the importance of having faith: "Listen to what the unjust judge says. And will not God bring about justice for his chosen ones, who cry out to him day and night? Will he keep putting them off? I tell you, he will see that they get justice, and quickly. However, when the Son of Man comes, will he find faith on the earth?" (Luke 18:6–8).

If you are not seeing miracles and the spiritual breakthrough you desire, perhaps you need to uncomplicate your life. Maybe you need to simplify your paradigm and rid yourself of the many distractions that keep you from having a holistic worldview.

My prayer is that when Christ returns, he will find faith in our hearts just as he is finding it in the millions of people around the world who genuinely and wholeheartedly place their trust in him. As we apply the lessons we've learned in this chapter and meditate on God's voice, I say to you, *become what you believe!*

If you find it difficult to have faith, yet you have a desire to believe, I offer you a prayer as a starting point in your journey. Find a place where you can be alone. Take a few moments to clear your mind of the pressures of your day, and pray the following prayer aloud. In the coming days and weeks, be aware of the answers that God will send your way. I believe miracles will come, because God wants to show himself to you in wonderful ways.

> *Father, I thank you for the opportunity to build my faith. I do not want to struggle with unbelief. I want to believe. I want to develop spiritual eyes to see your mighty hand at work. Help me overcome my unbelief. Give me your perspective, and grant me the ability to see the spiritual world around me. Throughout this process, open my eyes to recognize your will.*
>
> *Give me the ability to believe that you will do what seems to be impossible. Give me clarity when there is confusion. Grant me the same faith that the disciples had two thousand years ago. Bring people into my life that will lift my level of faith in a way that pleases you. I don't want to be manipulated, but I do want to see what is genuinely of you. Give me eyes to see and ears to hear. In Christ's name. Amen.*

Questions for discussion or personal reflection

1. Do you believe that demons, angels, and other principalities exist?

2. In what way do you believe that these beings impact the natural world? In your opinion, does the material world impact the supernatural world?

3. Can you identify a person in your life who has a healthy way of viewing the natural and supernatural world? Might they serve as a good role model for you?

4. In what way do you see the world differently from people who lived during the time of Christ? Do you believe we view the world more accurately today than did the New Testament writers?

5. How has your Western mindset derailed or deluded your faith in God? What are some of the ways you can refocus your faith today?

Chapter Two
URGENCY AND DESPERATION

The desperate man found himself standing at the back of the lot where one of my mentors, Carlos Annacondia, shared a message about how Jesus could heal us from any sickness. The man listened to the evangelist read the story in John 5 about the paralyzed man who sat for thirty-eight long years at the Pool of Bethesda.

Years before this night of the campaign, this man worked for a shipping company in Argentina. When he contracted an incurable disease, his employers gave him his pension, an early retirement, and sent him on a trip around the world. His only responsibility was to enjoy the ports of call. The ship came to a port in Israel, and he decided to disembark and see some of the Holy Land sites.

There he found a group of Spanish-speaking tourists listening to a guide share the history of the different archeological sites. He joined the group and followed them to the historical site where Jesus healed the paralyzed man at the Pool of Bethesda. The guide explained how an angel would descend and cause a whirlpool to churn the water. After this, the first person to enter the pool would be healed of whatever sickness he or she had. When the man heard the story, he said to himself, "If Jesus was here and healed the paralytic, surely this soil contains the power to heal. If miracles happened here, there is hope for me." So when no one was looking, he stooped down, grabbed a rock next to the pool, and slipped it into his pocket.

Later, when he returned to the ship, he proceeded to rub the rock over his entire body. He rubbed until his skin became raw, covered with abrasions and scratch marks. But his condition never got better. In fact, over time, it worsened. As the years passed, the man needed crutches to get around. It became apparent that the rock from the Pool of Bethesda did not make a difference at all. It didn't have any power.

As the man continued to stand at the back of the lot at the campaign, Carlos said, "Today, there are no miracles at the Pool of Bethesda. The angel doesn't descend and cause the waters to churn. No one receives healing there." The man nodded his head in agreement. *Carlos is right!* he thought. *That pool has no power. I'm living proof of that*. Then Carlos continued, "That's because God raised up someone greater than the angel and the pool itself. His name is Jesus of Nazareth, and he comes to bring healing to your life today. Seek him, not for what he can do for you but for who he is. He is the source of life, love, salvation, and hope for humanity."

The doctors recently had told the man he would be confined to a wheelchair for the rest of his life. He was desperate for a solution and was running out of time. One hundred fifty yards from the base of the platform, he began walking forward with one of his crutches lifted high in the air. He said, "Jesus, if it's true that you are the source of life, love, salvation, and hope for humanity, I want to receive from you tonight." Seven days later, the same man ran up the stairs of the platform jumping, praising, and worshiping the Lord. He shared with the crowd the miraculous story you just read. He was completely healed, and the doctors declared that his disease had disappeared from his body. He came to the campaign that night in a state of urgency and desperation, and God responded to him with miracle-working power.

How Desperation Can Be a Blessing

The third characteristic found in those who experience the miraculous is a sense of *urgency and desperation*. People experience miracles in other countries because they are desperate for them. They have an urgency that drives them to knock on heaven's door until they receive an answer. Their options are few. Their resources are scarce. Their time is limited. All these factors drive them to their knees. In areas where they have nowhere to run except to God, it's no wonder they have the faith that moves his hand.

It's important to note that many African, Latin American, and Asian believers have a definition of desperation that is much more true to the definition than ours. When we send a text message that must go through, we think that's desperate. When we must arrive at an appointment or suffer the consequences of an angry boss, we believe that's desperate. When we weigh ourselves trying to lose the last five pounds before an important engagement, we feel that's desperate. When we stand in line for nine hours waiting to purchase the latest smartphone on the day of its release, it seems desperate. When a cruise ship loses power in the middle of the ocean and passengers are forced to use red hazard bags because the onboard toilets no longer work, we are sure that's desperate. But our brothers and sisters in other cultures often have a different understanding of desperation.

On February 15, 2013, a meteor weighing more than the Eiffel Tower and traveling 41,000 mph entered the earth's atmosphere and exploded as it entered into Russian air space. The airburst and debris trail generated a light brighter than the sun. The eleven-thousand-ton rock streaked across the sky until it crashed into Lake Chebarkul. The shockwave caused damage to over 7,200 buildings in six different cities. Over 1,490 injured people sought medical attention. The energy released was approximately 440 kilotons of TNT, twenty-five times more than the atomic bomb detonated over Hiroshima.[1] Although the meteor impacted tens of thousands of lives, the American media spent little time covering this catastrophic event. Why? Because in the minds of news producers, a much more important story of desperation was developing in the Caribbean.

They spent several days covering the cruise ship Carnival Triumph as it was being towed back to port after a small engine fire rendered it powerless off the coast of Mexico. The number-one topic of discussion was how uncomfortable it must have been for many of the passengers to sleep on deck and be inconvenienced to the point of having to use red biohazard bags instead of the onboard toilets.[2] Both news stories broke the same week, but only one dominated U.S. news cycles.

I called a friend in Costa Rica and mentioned that I hadn't heard much of what was happening in Russia because of what was happening the Caribbean. He couldn't believe it. He replied, "What took place in Russia was an apocalyptic event! It's all over the news down here. Our hearts hurt for those poor people struck by this tragedy." What a contrast between the two worldviews. Our definition of desperation and urgency greatly differs from the rest of the world.

Not only do we define desperation differently than many believers in Africa, Asia, and Latin America, but we also have greater access to resources than they. They don't always have a plethora of doctors to choose from or insurance policies to pay the bills for the best medical care. Their lack of access to resources creates in them a dependency on God, much like those who lived in the New Testament.

Imagine there is no cure for your disease. Imagine there are no hospitals, no doctors, no pain medication, no wheelchairs, and no hope to generate any income. That was the life of one man who was confined to a cot. One morning, four of his friends came by his home and carried him a significant distance to see a healer. They had heard about Jesus and how God was using him to heal the sick. So they decided to take their friend to see Jesus.

When the group arrived at the home, they discovered an overwhelming crowd of people already there listening to Jesus' teaching. There was no way to squeeze by the hundreds of people pressing in to have contact with the Lord. In this story found in Luke 5:17–26, Luke pauses his narration to make it clear that the power of the Lord was with Jesus to heal. In spite of the huge obstacle of the crowd, the four men had a strong sense of urgency. Their desperation was over the top. Instead of giving up, they did the unexpected. They hoisted their friend up the outside of the house, tore apart the roof directly over the Savior's head, and lowered the man to the feet of Jesus.

Luke did not say, "When Jesus saw their urgency or desperation . . ." Instead he writes, "When Jesus saw their *faith,*" he said, "friend, your sins are forgiven." Faith is manifested many times in our desperate actions, which drive us to pull apart a roof, walk twenty miles through the jungle, and even break social norms to get God's attention. Frankly, I seldom meet anyone in Western civilization with such tenacity as the four men mentioned in Luke's Gospel.

Interestingly, when the Pharisees heard the Lord's comments, they began to question in their hearts, "Who can forgive sins but God alone?" (Luke 5:21). The conversation between the paralyzed man and Jesus abruptly stops as Jesus' attention is now diverted to deal with the religious leaders and their self-righteous attitude disguised as theological questions. Many times in our churches today, God wants to do the miraculous. He wants to help the hurting, the marginalized, and the oppressed. But instead, he has to deal with *religious* people who insist on beating the same theological drums the Pharisees did two thousand years ago. The spirit of religiosity and Phariseeism can bring paralysis to our churches and our life of faith.

Jesus brings the story to a conclusion when he says, "Why are you thinking these things in your hearts? Which is easier: to say, 'Your sins are forgiven,' or to say, 'Get up and walk'? But that you may know that the Son of Man has authority on earth to forgive sins . . ." He speaks to the paralyzed man, "I tell you, get up, take your mat and go home" (Luke 5:22–24). Immediately, the man stood up in front of everyone, grabbed his mat, and began to walk out of the crowded house. Meanwhile, his four friends watched through the hole in the roof they had made for the friend they loved. Their desperation and urgency pushed them to the limits. It pushed them to do something that they would not do under normal conditions. Their faith as defined in this story caused them to knock on heaven's door until they got an answer.

How desperate are we for a miracle? How many choices do we have if God doesn't give us what we need? It's difficult to sense urgency or desperation when we have limitless options. Today, we have healthcare and medical insurance policies. We have life insurance, dental insurance, car insurance, renter's insurance, and fire insurance. We can even take out policies on our body parts if we desire. We can take out policies on someone else's life. In the United States alone, we have over 5,700 hospitals, 624,434 medical practitioners, and over 2.8 million registered nurses. All of these wonderful advances in medicine, although beneficial, build a wall of protection that slowly erodes our dependency on God and shifts our dependency to man-made systems and bureaucracies. Dependence on these man-made systems eliminates our sense of urgency and desperation. Obviously, people in the New Testament would find the concept of so much protection incomprehensible. So would most of the world outside of Western Europe and North America today, where people live much closer to the urgency and desperation of those during the New Testament period.

You may wonder if I have insurance for my home and car? Or if I have a healthcare policy for my family? Absolutely! Do I think you should too? Of course, if you can afford it. Let me also add that I take blood pressure and cholesterol medication. You see, my faith tells me that unless God has engineered my DNA to work with a one-size-fits-all medicine, I will develop cardiovascular disease. So even though I take the pills, I depend on God for an ongoing miracle.

Let me underscore that insurance, medication, and advances in technology are wonderful. However, I am fully aware that God is sovereign, and ultimately, my life rests in his hands. I am also aware that our man-made systems tend to pull me away from a dependence upon the Lord. As we discussed in chapter 1, our Western systems fragment my worldview. There is good news, though. Although the challenge might seem daunting, there is hope for those of us who live in the twenty-first century and who desire to lead a life of faith.

A Model for Developing Urgency and Desperation

The young fisherman, Simon, worked out on the Sea of Galilee every night. His business was doing fairly well. He had several boats, several partners, a home, a wife, and children. One day, Jesus was walking along the shore when he approached Simon and his brother Andrew and said, "Come, follow me, . . . and I will make you fishers of men" (Matt. 4:19). I'm sure it was challenging for Simon to leave his assets and the trade he worked so hard to develop, but he managed to heed the call and became one of Jesus' disciples.

Then in John 6 we find an interesting exchange between Jesus and his disciples. He throws down the gauntlet with this graphic statement: "I tell you the truth, unless you eat the flesh of the Son of Man and drink his blood, you have no life in you" (v. 53). In verse 60 we see their response. The large group of disciples began to grumble and said to one another, "This is a hard teaching. Who can accept it?" Jesus responds with a question, "Does this offend you? What if you see the Son of Man ascend to where he was before! The Spirit gives life; the flesh counts for nothing. The words I have spoken to you are spirit and they are life. Yet there are some of you who do not believe" (John 6:61–64).

Continuing the story in verse 66, we find that "from this time many of his disciples turned back and no longer followed him". Seeing that the multitudes were turning away, Jesus asked the twelve, "You do not want to leave too, do you?" They had laid down everything for him. Were there really any other options? Did they have any other legitimate choice? Simon, now called Peter, immediately responds with decisive words of affirmation: "Lord, to whom shall we go? You have the words of eternal life. We believe and know that you are the Holy One of God" (vv. 68–69). Peter made a choice to be desperate. He chose to depend on and follow the Lord. He wasn't born desperate, but he chose to keep the fires of urgency in his heart. He realized that of all the things in life upon which we can become dependent, choosing to lean on God is the wisest and most appropriate choice.

You may have several hundred million dollars in the bank, with perfect health and angels for children. Maybe your marriage is flawless, and your mother-in-law is a saint. Your life is seemingly perfect. These things do not last either here or in eternity. Consequently, placing your unwavering faith in God and not on the pieces of your life is the wisest choice you can make. Latin Americans, Asians, and Africans who have New Testament faith know that what Jesus said is true. "The Spirit gives life; the flesh counts for nothing" (John 6:63). They know that sooner or later we will all need God. Our lives are in his hands. So if you want to choose to live a life of New Testament faith, *choose to be desperate* and see God's agenda as urgent. Peter's testimony shows us, first of all, that faithful people choose to be dependent on God. Being desperate for God is a choice.

Second, recognize that as a society, we've grown overly dependent on our own capabilities, technology, knowledge, and the firewalls that protect us. These things give us a sense of security that cannot be proven or substantiated. They are not as reliable as we think. Whether we want to admit it or not, our systems have limitations, and they cannot bring redemption, salvation, or deliverance. Only God can. God may use a doctor, medicine, technology, or a specific procedure to bring us healing. He may perform a miracle through others. The point is, he is the one who decides how he will respond to our need. Our job is simply to knock on heaven's door until the answer comes. God is our starting point. He is our source. Ultimately, he is our solution. That's the way our friends overseas see the hand of God working.

Third, we need to realize that we will be dead much longer than we are alive. The physical world is temporal. It's here to-day and gone tomorrow. So our awareness of the supernatural must play a much more prominent role in how we view our op-tions. We must grab hold of what our friends in other countries see, that God is the author and finisher of life. He is the creator, and we are the creation. He calls the shots and, ultimately, he is responsible for the well-being of those who place their trust in him.

I wrote a story that illustrates these three points in my book *Power to Reinvent Yourself*. It's worth sharing the story here.

The first night of our first open-air outreach was held in a marginalized community filled with poverty, gangs, prostitu-tion, and drugs. At the end of the message, we gave an invita-tion for people to receive prayer for healing. The very first per-son for whom we prayed was an eight-year-old little girl. Her name was Vivian. Her grandmother was nudging her forward determined to have our team pray for her.

I leaned down and asked the bright-eyed scared little girl how we might be of assistance. Before she could open her mouth, her grandmother spoke up with authority. "We took her to the clinic earlier today, and the doctors determined that she has curvature of the spine. She's missing three ribs. Unless we operate, she will be an invalid. This is unacceptable. I've come with faith, because we need a miracle. We don't have the money to pay for an operation. We're desperate for God to do something!"

I knelt down on one knee and asked Vivian, "Well, sweet-heart, do you believe the Lord can heal you?" She nodded with-out saying a word. After praying for her, we continued down the line of people waiting patiently for prayer. At the end of the evening, I felt a tug on the back of my jacket. I turned around, and there stood Vivian. I said, "Well, hello. How can I help you?"

She said, "I believe the Lord has healed me."

At that moment, this eight-year-old little girl presented an overwhelming challenge to my way of thinking. I considered myself a person of faith. After all, I just finished praying for three hundred people, believing that God would do something miraculous in their lives. Still, the skeptic in me wanted proof. My American paradigm wanted a doctor to sign off on anything before I believed it. I simply responded, "Oh that's wonderful sweetheart." But you and I know what that means. As adults we know how to say something without saying much at all, but God knows what's truly in our hearts. People who doubt say, "Seeing is believing." People of faith say, "Believing is seeing."

As soon as those words dropped out of my mouth, I looked over and spotted a physician who happened to be attending the campaign that night. I walked over and said, "Hello doctor. There's a little girl over here who tells me that she's received a miracle."

He interrupted, "Oh that's Vivian. I examined her earlier today at the clinic. She's missing three ribs. Unless we operate, she's going to be an invalid."

I said, "Well, she tells me that God miraculously touched her spine."

He said, "I can verify that if you wish."

He walked over to her and requested to look at her back once again. He lifted her shirt as she bent over with her hands on her knees. As he counted her ribs by twos from her neck down her spine, he suddenly paused. His mouth opened slightly as his eyebrows shot to the top of his forehead. "This is not the same back that I looked at this morning. There was an obvious gaping hole, but it is now gone. The ribs that were missing are there." Vivian reached out and hugged her grandmother who broke out in tears. I was speechless.

When Vivian's grandmother initially heard the sad news earlier that day, she could have said, "Well, I'll have to go back to work. I'll save every dime, and we'll get that operation that she needs!" Or "I'll raise money, ask people to give, and do whatever it takes." Sincerely, I would say that she would have been more than justified. But that wasn't her first reaction. Her first impulse was to seek God's intervention and divine healing. She didn't have any options. She didn't have any resources. She had God. That first reaction is the way people overseas are spiritually wired.[3]

As people of faith, our worldview should always be to enjoy the advances that God has allowed us to experience with a grateful heart. But we should never think, *I'll pray, and if that doesn't work, I can always try doctor A. Then if that doesn't pan out, I'll try option B, and then move on to remedy C*. Our faith should lead us to think, *I'll pray, and if God doesn't heal me instantly, he'll lead me to his next remedy for my life whether that's doctor A or option B*. With the eyes of faith we can see how God orchestrates every step of our lives when we place our trust in him, regardless of how many man-made resources we have at our disposal.

On more than one occasion, Jesus dealt with Simon Peter about trusting God to meet his needs. In Mark 1, the Lord called him to leave his fishing business. Then in Luke 5:1–11, Jesus had to reiterate that call a second time after the miraculous catch of fish. In Matthew 17:24–27, the Lord miraculously provided a four-drachma coin in the mouth of a fish to pay the temple tax. After Jesus performed all the miracles, died, and rose from the dead, Peter went back to his old profession (John 21:4–14). It took a heart-to-heart chat with the risen Christ on the beach for Peter to finally understand that he could count on God. Eventually, the Lord brought Peter to completely depend on him. It's true that Peter's faith ebbed and flowed. He struggled throughout his developmental years as a Christian. Through it all, though, he made the choice to be desperate, dependent, and to have a sense of urgency for God.

So how much do you depend on God? How desperate are you for his presence, his solution, his redeeming power? Do you knock on heaven's door until you get an answer? Or do you instead rely on man-made systems and the many options we have in the twenty-first century?

Several years ago, I walked into the largest soccer stadium at the time in Costa Rica. We were kicking off the four-night crusade that was the culmination of several years of preparation. Hundreds of people, donors, and team members from churches all over the globe flew in to take part in the historic event. We were hoping for twenty-five thousand people, but after a torrential downpour earlier that afternoon, it seemed only a fraction of that number would attend that first night. Sure enough, when we started, there were six thousand people. That may seem like an astronomical number, but when you're expecting four times as many people, it is depressing.

There I sat in the green room having a pity party. I asked myself the question that sooner or later we all ask ourselves, "What am I doing with my life?" Finally, the president of the pastors' alliance walked in, encouraged me, and said, "Do what

God called you to do! We're here to support you." Buoyed by his words, I went out and preached with all of my conviction. I gave an invitation and watched fifteen hundred people come forward for salvation. At the end of the altar call, I noticed someone jumping over the barricades, evading the security team, and briskly coming up the stairs to the stage. She was a young woman about twenty years of age. I looked at the two security officers who had been positioned next to the barricade to ensure that this sort of thing wouldn't happen in the middle of the time of ministry. They shrugged their shoulders as if to say, "I don't know how she got up there."

The young lady was now walking toward me on the platform. She said, "Jason, don't you recognize me?" I said, "I am sorry, I don't." She said, "It's me, Vivian." I paused for five long seconds, remembering the little girl who was healed of a spinal defect, and said, "Vivian!? Wow, you've changed. You're all grown up. And I can see that you have no physical ailments." She replied, "May I have the microphone? These wonderful people need to hear about the great things God can do."

As this chapter comes to a close, you may notice that I have not suggested that people experience miracles because of persecution. A majority of Jesus' miracles happened when things were going well. Sure, he faced opposition, but the recipients of his miracles didn't face persecution. Today, in the areas of the world where miracles occur, people may or may not face opposition. The point is they don't have many options. Thus, they turn to God and place their hope in him.

Poverty isn't a reason people experience the miraculous either. Both rich and poor people throughout Latin America, Africa, and Asia experience miracles and healings. Rich and poor people who experience the miraculous have something in common. They're desperate. God's hand moves when people desperately and persistently seek him. Just like Peter did when he stated with confidence, "Where else can we go? You alone have the words of eternal life!"

Make the choice to be desperate for God's presence. Keep the urgency fresh in your spirit. Don't settle for a man-made version of peace of mind that sooner or later is bound to fail. Push aside all the distractions, and remember that your life is ultimately in God's hands. Friend, I want you to be encouraged and inspired to *become what you believe!*

To help you in that quest, I've written out a simple prayer that can serve as a guide. May it help you connect with the Lord in order for you to become more desperate for him.

Lord, I ask your forgiveness for not putting you in first place in my life. My urgency and dependence on you has been clouded by all of the options that society offers. You are my source of life. You are my solution. You uphold me with your righteous right hand. Help me to see that you're at work in every detail of my life.

I know that you hold all things together, and that nothing in the universe moves forward without you. So help me to see that ultimately, my life rests in your hands. I want to be desperate for your presence, and I want to depend on you. In Christ's name. Amen.

Questions for discussion or personal reflection

1. In what ways are you solely dependent on God for a miracle? In what ways are you completely self-sufficient?

2. In what ways do you feel completely safe and secure from tragedy? What are some of the firewalls in your life that protect you from pain and suffering?

3. How can you become more dependent on God? Is there a way you can choose to depend on him although you have all your needs met? If so, how?

4. What do you believe is a healthy balance between being responsible for your well-being and being dependent on the Lord for his provision?

Chapter Three
PERSUADED BEFORE THE ENCOUNTER

Rosa's alarm clock sounded at 2:30 a.m. The thirty-eight-year-old mother of three rubbed her eyes, sat up, and immediately got dressed for what would be a very long day. For several months, she had been planning to take her family to a Christian crusade, with a profound conviction that an encounter with Christ would change their lives forever. She was convinced that Jesus was their only solution.

The task was challenging, though. Her mother refused to fly. So to ensure that the family (her sister, brother-in-law, mother, niece, and nephew) would arrive without incident, she drove four hundred miles to pick them up by 10:00 a.m. Then she drove another 170 miles in the opposite direction to the crusade venue, overcoming traffic delays, a flat tire, and carsickness. In the meantime, her husband drove their three children the 230-mile distance from their home to the crusade.

Rosa and the other five arrived at the stadium minutes before the event began. Her husband and their three children were waiting just inside the main tunnel entrance. As they entered the arena, an usher waved them over. Surprisingly, he had spotted ten empty seats in the second row and guided them to the area twenty feet from the stage. During the children's outreach, Rosa's niece and nephew raised their hands indicating they wanted to begin a relationship with Christ. So Rosa escorted them to the open area in front of the stage.

After an intermission and a time of worship, I shared a message and gave an invitation for people to accept Christ. I remember Rosa walking forward with three other family members.

Each one had a hand raised. Tears streamed down her sister's face. She could barely contain her brokenness. Her brother-in-law, a humble auto mechanic, began to cry as well. That night, he realized that if he were going to live a life acceptable to God, he needed to submit to Christ's lordship. Even Rosa's mother occasionally wiped a tear from her eyes. No one was more ecstatic than Rosa, whose tears revealed her overwhelming sense of gratitude to God. She knew that God honored her faith. All three of Rosa's relatives prayed the prayer of salvation, asking Jesus into their hearts to start a new life in them. That day, a miracle took place. The entire family gave their hearts to Christ and experienced salvation for the first time.

When Rosa finally pulled into her driveway, she had driven a total of 1,180 miles, and it took her twenty-five hours to do it. She spent two hundred dollars in gas, which was fifteen percent of her monthly salary. She made an extraordinary effort so that her family could have an encounter with Christ.

One month later, she wrote me a letter sharing this story. She said, "My heart is overwhelmed with joy and appreciation. I prayed for them for a decade and a half. I carried a burden for them for years. I prepared for the event for months. Although we faced many barriers, I knew that if we could have an encounter with God, he would release his power and my family would experience salvation." Rosa was convinced well before the encounter that Christ was the only solution for her family, and God honored her faith. Today, all of them continue to serve the Lord in their local church.

The Miracle Has Already Begun

The third characteristic found in those who experience the

miraculous is simply this. People are *convinced that Christ is their solution before their encounter with him*. Notice that I do not use the words *feeling, sense,* or even *hope*. It's not a question of hope. It's a conviction. It's not a question of an aspiration or desire. It's almost a certainty.

In the same way, people in the New Testament were already persuaded before they met Jesus face to face. In the four Gospels, there are ten instances where each writer states that people had previously heard of Jesus' power, and were convinced he was their solution. Their actions, demeanor, and words strongly indicate this. In each case, people are convinced before they have any contact with Christ.

Matthew 20:30, Mark 3:8–10, Mark 7:25, Mark 10:47, Luke 6:17–19, Luke 7:3, John 4:47, and John 12:18 are wonderful verses that demonstrate this truth. Luke 5:15 sums it up this way: "Yet the news about him spread all the more, so that crowds of people came to hear him and to be healed of their sicknesses." Of all the people in the New Testament, however, the woman who had been bleeding for twelve long years, whose story is told in Mark 5:25–34, personifies someone who was completely convinced of Jesus' power prior to meeting him.

Mark tells a marvelous story within a story in chapter 5 of his Gospel. It's set up as Jairus, a synagogue ruler, begs Jesus to come with him and heal his ailing daughter. So Jesus decides to go. Suddenly, the storyline takes a detour when a woman is introduced into the narrative. She was among those in the crowd who were following Christ. Her sickness was a severe case of hemorrhaging. Mark tells us that she had suffered under the care of many doctors, which suggests that some of them had used questionable practices and perhaps even experimented on her. For more than a decade, she tried treatment after treatment, and instead of getting better, her condition only grew worse.

People caught in this type of vicious cycle often do not grow in faith nor do they become optimistic. Eventually, their sickness becomes their identity. For this woman, however, that is not what happens.

After describing her affliction, Mark uses the phrase that is central to our discussion: *when she heard about Jesus*. Immediately following these words is the result of what her spirit heard. Years of disillusionment and the social norms that keep an unclean woman at bay suddenly shatter as she comes up behind Jesus in the crowd and touches his cloak. She believes in her heart, "If I just touch his clothes, I will be healed."

Like a lightning bolt, the power of God explodes out of Jesus, and immediately her bleeding stops. There is no doubt—she knows that she is completely healed. She wasn't the only one who felt the healing power, though. Jesus did, too. The woman's faith flipped the switch and activated the power of God that set her free. But now, Jesus wants to know who did this without his permission. He turns to the crowd and asks, "Who touched my clothes?"

The disciples don't understand the question because they see scores of people pressing in and touching him. Jesus keeps looking for the individual who received the healing. Perhaps he didn't expect the person to be a woman or even an unclean woman. Maybe she was hiding in the crowd. Whatever the case, she knew that she had to come clean and tell him what happened. So she came and fell at his feet, trembling with fear and confessed everything. Jesus looked at her and said, "Daughter, your faith has healed you. Go in peace and be freed from your suffering" (Mark 5:34). Jesus does not mention the power of God that healed her. Instead he asserts that it was her faith that moved the hand of God.

I would add an additional observation. Her miracle did not begin when she touched Jesus' garment. It began when she heard about Jesus. It started when she believed he was the solution, well before her encounter with him. If you read this story in the original language, you will see that Mark leaves no room for doubt. In the mind of the woman, she never questions from the time she heard about Jesus until her bleeding stopped. The only conditional language used in the text is this: "If I just touch his clothes." The only barrier, at least in her mind, was getting close enough to touch Jesus' cloak.

When Gossip Is Godly

In many parts of Latin America, Africa, and Asia, believers have a deep conviction that Christ can meet every need they have. Regardless of the barrier, they are convinced that God is the answer. One of the reasons this is so widespread is that they hear constant reports of miraculous things happening everywhere. They have friends and neighbors who share personal stories about how God heals the sick, sets people free from bondage, binds up the brokenhearted, saves the lost, gives people a reason to live, and solves impossible problems. It's no wonder when people hear these personal and inspirational stories, their faith grows.

If I hear something unfounded and negative about you and I share that information with someone else, that is gossip. However, if I hear that you've experienced a miraculous remedy that glorifies God and I share that with someone, that is godly gossip. Imagine entire neighborhoods talking about a drug dealer being set free by the power of God. Imagine the family celebration that takes place when a mother is healed of breast cancer. Imagine a significant percentage of a continent talking about miracles, healings, and divine wonders. That is precisely what is happening in many parts of the world today. The reports build greater expectancy, and faith in God spreads like wildfire.

In evangelistic campaigns around the world, ministers use a Bible verse that captures this concept: "So then faith comes by hearing, and hearing by the word of God" (Rom. 10:17, NKJV). According to *Strong's Greek Dictionary,* the Greek word *rhēma* has several different meanings, such as an utterance (individually, collectively or specially); by implication, a matter or topic (especially of narration, command or dispute).[1] Some versions of *Strong's* include a thing spoken, (a) a word or saying of any kind, as command, report, promise, (b) a thing, matter, business.[2]

I find these definitions interesting, especially the word *report*. In light of this definition, the phrase has a slightly different nuance, "So then faith comes by hearing, and hearing the *report* of God."

Good reports inspire more faith and thus produce more miracles. If miracles happen yet no one reports on them, faith does not build and fewer people are inspired. Again, some might argue, "God does miracles all the time. We just need to take notice." I agree. But if no one talks about them, the quantity of miracles begins to decline because fewer people are inspired. This is precisely what is happening in North America and Western Europe.

The Power of Testimony

There are areas of the world where we can hear testimonies in every worship service. African and Latin American believers, for example, need no excuse to proclaim the miracle that God did in their lives that week. When these reports are given, people respond with cheers and applause. Their faith is inspired, and in turn it produces more miracles because their expectancy rises.

It is well known that people in other cultures value time differently than we in the West do. They are not as concerned about a church service running over thirty minutes or an hour on occasion. Time may not be the issue here, though. North Americans will arrive at a theater a half hour early to catch every preview, then sit through a three-hour movie. They will arrive at the airport two-and-a-half hours early for their flight. People become fidgety when church doesn't end on time because, just like a movie, they know how it's going to end. However, when we hear testimonies for the first time from people we know, it creates a whole new level of excitement. In those circumstances, people don't know how it will end and are glad to stay to find out. And their faith grows.

Personal testimonies are vital to the life of local churches. In fact, they are one of the greatest contributing factors to reaching new people, as well as keeping the seasoned veterans motivated and enthused. Testimonies are just as important as music or an eloquent sermon. Why? Because they give legitimacy to the sermon and to the songs we sing. Testimonies are real evidence that God is indeed working in our midst. They show that what God proclaims in his Word is not just philosophy or theory. Testimonies show that God interacts with humanity and demonstrates his love in everyday life.

The problem we face today in many of our churches in North America and Western Europe is that we rarely hear any reports of God's activity in our lives. I cannot tell you the last time I saw someone in our culture invited to give his or her testimony in church. Occasionally, I see a well-produced video testimony on a large projection screen. Don't get me wrong. I appreciate good production, but testimonies have their greatest affect when people we know personally stand up and say, "Listen to the miracle that God did in my life this week."

I'm aware that many pastors and lay people argue that there isn't enough time in a service to listen to people's unfiltered ramblings. Who knows what people will say if they're given a microphone? Even worse, someone may say something that is doctrinally questionable. Sure, people might ramble or say something questionable, but considering what little spiritual activity takes place in many of our houses of worship, stirring up the waters may be a good thing.

Where are the growing churches throughout the world? Where is revival breaking out? It certainly isn't in Western Europe or North America. Why is that? From this missionary's perspective, it's because our people are not testifying. They don't report on God's activity. As a result, others are not inspired, and their faith is not being built up. The word (report) isn't spreading, and so faith doesn't come. Instead, people in our churches are in maintenance mode. We are growing old and stagnant, spiritually speaking.

I want to suggest four things you can do to create godly gossip through the power of the testimony. When godly gossip occurs, inevitably people's faith will grow, and like believers around the world, the people you impact will be convinced that Jesus is their solution.

First, look for ways to proclaim the great things God is doing in your life. Begin to spread the report. Be a good gossiper. Don't worry about sounding polished. Genuineness trumps first-rate production every time. Christians in Latin America, Africa, and Asia are less concerned with looking professional. They are much more concerned about being authentic and genuine.

Second, testimonies should glorify God and not the local church or parachurch ministry. A testimony should never be a church marketing campaign. I have seen this too many times, especially in the last decade in North America. People can spot mixed motives. They can recognize a public relations campaign when they see one. Whenever our motive for testifying is to make our ministry more popular or make our church bigger, we tread on thin ice. The Lord will not share the glory, and he detests it when people build their own empires under the auspices of the Kingdom of God. Nor should testimonies be about how attending church makes us better people. Church doesn't transform our lives, God does. The power of God revolutionizes us, and the church is an instrument to accomplish that task. Look for testimonies that demonstrate God's power and ones that give him the glory.

Further, in the last two decades, people have become skeptical of those they do not know. I distinctly remember having a conversation with someone in 1994 on this topic. This person was rather dogmatic and felt that church should be more like a movie experience, with little interaction aside from congregational singing. I replied, "Nothing encourages people more than when they hear testimonies of those who have been healed, delivered, or saved." She argued, "I don't feel comfortable turning a church service into a show! Whenever you parade people on stage showing off something that can't be verified, you make it seem like a televangelist production." She obviously was reacting to something she saw on television and felt that those involved were disingenuous. This is why hearing testimonies from those we know are much more effective than slick pre-packaged presentations.

Third, try to institute a time in the worship service for people to share their personal testimonies. Again, testimonies don't have to be perfect. They simply need to be genuine. New Testament believers were wired to share how Jesus transformed their lives and they did so in a genuine way. They knew how to communicate their story to reach the common Jew and Gentile. Latino believers do the same thing, as do Africans and Asians, and they are experts at describing the *before* and *after*.

Recently, I spoke at Saddleback Church in Lake Forest, California. Even though my background is different than that of Pastor Rick Warren, he asked me to preach all five services in English and Spanish. Prior to speaking there, I attended a service at his church on Father's Day and noticed that Pastor Warren weaved four different salvation testimonies into his message. Four dads got up and told the story of how they gave their hearts to Christ. It's no wonder Saddleback is one of the largest churches in America. A church that encourages its people to share their personal testimony on a consistent basis cannot help but experience growth.

Fourth, we all need to learn the art of giving our testimony. Occasionally, I coach corporate speakers in how to tell their signature story more effectively. A signature story is the one personal episode that we share better than any other, and it illustrates how we got to where we are in life.

I tell corporate speakers that when they tell their signature story they should describe the *before*. The listener wants to know what life was like before transformation took place. Often this includes a brief summary of one's family life growing up. It might also touch on a dark chapter before change occurred.

In addition, I tell speakers to describe the *transformational moment*. Every listener wants to hear what it was like when they experienced the *A-ha* moment, the miracle, or breakthrough.

Then I tell them to describe the *after*. I want to hear how their life has been revolutionized as a result of what took place. I want to hear how their relationships, health, feelings, and direction in life have all changed.

Finally, I want them to explain how what happened to them can transform *my life*. When people share their testimony in a worship service or a secular setting and they say the words, "If my life can change as a result of ________ (fill in the blank), your life can change too!", I know that they will have an impact on many lives. That is the function of a testimony.

The Power of the Decision

One of the questions I am asked often is, why do people experience miracles in meetings where a preacher or ministry has a questionable reputation? I want to offer two answers to this question. First, people come to meetings expecting something. They come with faith, and they've already decided that they'll experience something miraculous before they arrive at the meeting. They are convinced that Christ has the solution they need. In this light, when people place their sincere faith in God, the instrument that he chooses to use becomes irrelevant.

This is true in Latin America and in other parts of the world. They believe that as soon as they have contact with God, his power will begin to work in their lives. They are already convinced that he holds the solution, and it's that confidence in the

Lord that causes miracles to happen. I can tell you that we've seen hundreds upon hundreds of miracles happen in campaigns we've held around the world. I couldn't tell you if my faith had anything to do with it. I can say confidently that people in Latin America come with a great level of expectancy, and I see that quality more often than not when miracles occur in the New Testament.

Second, the Bible says,

> As the rain and the snow come down from heaven, and do not return to it without watering the earth and making it bud and flourish, so that it yields seed for the sower and bread for the eater, so is my word that goes out from my mouth: It will not return to me empty, but will accomplish what I desire and achieve the purpose for which I sent it. (Isa. 55:10–11)

God's Word doesn't return void. It produces miracles. It produces godly things in us. The sower's job is to sow, but the sower can't change or dilute the power of God's Word. This is good news for all of us. The miracle of salvation, healing, and deliverance doesn't depend on the person who sows. It depends on the seed and soil. If the sower does his or her job, even while struggling with sin, ultimately, the seed provides the DNA for what will grow. The human heart is the soil in which the seed germinates, grows, and eventually produces fruit. While it's true that every individual who wants to sow must strive to have a pure and clean heart, God will still "accomplish what he desires and achieve the purpose for which he sends" the seed.

The essence of this chapter centers on a decision. A decision carries people to an encounter with Christ where they find healing, redemption, and solution. So then, I want to encourage you to make a choice. Decide that Christ is the solution for your life, before anything else. Be convinced before your encounter that he has the answer and will always guide you to what is good. In order to be convinced, you must do what people around the world and those who lived during the time of Christ do—you must hear and believe the reports. If you don't hear the reports, how can you believe them? And if you don't believe the reports, how will faith grow in you? Like we learned in chapter 2, your desperation and urgency will cause you to seek. As you seek, choose to believe. Then, just like the woman with the issue of blood, reach out and touch his cloak!

Throughout the four Gospels, people heard about Jesus before they encountered him. The stories of healing, deliverance, and wonders were remarkable. News about Jesus spread throughout the nation and surrounding areas. Before people encountered him, they thought, *if he can heal the sick, deliver the oppressed, and bring hope to the hopeless, surely he has a solution for me*. Their hearts were prepared and convinced before they ever saw Jesus.

Throughout the areas of the world where miracles are prevalent today, people hear about the miraculous things that God does and they also choose to believe. Preachers inspire faith by talking about the miracles in the New Testament, and they encourage their people to share their stories in a number of settings. Just like the disciples, they boldly share the miraculous things that God does every opportunity they have. Like a snowball rolling down a hill, the momentum picks up, and the movement grows as the word spreads quickly.

I want you to experience spiritual breakthroughs, miracles, and revival. My prayer is that you experience the same power that those who walked with Jesus experienced two thousand years ago. I pray that you are convinced, persuaded, and inspired to seek Jesus before anything or anyone else so that you can *become what you believe!*

As you consider what we've learned in this chapter, we've come to the point where God can cement these truths in your heart. As you ponder the importance of the power of your decisions based upon the reports that you hear, ask God to help you be a good gossiper and someone who promotes the good things he is doing. If you need an example of a sincere prayer, the following has served me well in connecting my heart with the Lord's. Feel free to pray it aloud and remember to be conscious of the answer God sends in the coming days, weeks, and months.

Father, I ask you to open my eyes to see the powerful things you are doing in my life, family, community, and around the world. I pray that the reports would inspire faith in me so that I can become a believer. As I begin to recognize your mighty hand working in my life, help me to spread the word and inspire others.

I want to become someone of great faith. I want to see miracles, healings, deliverances, salvations, and revival. Use me. Open my eyes. Help me to glorify you in every legitimate way I can. I pray these things, choosing to believe that you are the solution. I ask you as someone choosing to believe that you have my answer. I pray this all in Christ's name. Amen.

Questions for discussion or personal reflection

1. List some of the ways gossip can be good.

2. In what ways does a testimony of someone you know inspire you?

3. How important is it to be convinced that Jesus is the solution prior to one's encounter with him? How important is hearing testimonies that impact your faith?

4. What are some of the things you can do to inspire faith in others? How can you build your faith?

Chapter Four

HONOR AND RESPECT FOR AUTHORITY

I pulled into the parking lot of a church in Southern California in an old Chevy pickup truck. I have no idea how Juan knew I was the keynote speaker for the evening's event. After all, my vehicle was not the typical keynote speaker's mode of transportation. Nevertheless, he approached my truck and asked, "Are you Jason Frenn?" I said, "Yes, I am." He said, "If you'll give me your keys, I'll handle everything from here." I said, "Oh, thank you. I appreciate your help, but please tell me, who are you?" He smiled and responded, "I'm Juan, a volunteer here at the church, and I'll make sure your book table is set up and that you have everything you need." He proceeded to unload my eight boxes of books, carry them into the church lobby, and lay them on the display table. When the service started, he was already sitting in the second row.

When I finished speaking in the service, I gave the altar call and asked if anyone needed prayer for healing. Juan raised his hand, then placed it on the lower portion of his back. We prayed together. After praying for the entire group who came forward, I asked the crowd, "Does anyone feel a difference in their body since the time they walked in the door?" Several people raised their hands, including Juan. He smiled and said, "¡Se me fue el dolor!" (The pain is gone!)

After the service, Juan assisted in the sale of my books, packed up what was left over, and carried everything back to my truck. He wouldn't even let me carry my own Bible. He insisted on serving me in every detail of my visit. Juan is not from the United States; he emigrated from Latin America.

North Americans are not used to receiving such service. In the back of our minds, we think that people want something in return for treating us so well. That makes us feel uncomfortable, because we don't want to feel indebted to anyone.

As we continue our journey to discover New Testament faith, the fourth characteristic found in those who experience the miraculous is a profound *respect and honor for spiritual authority.* Latin American, African, and Asian Christians demonstrate a deep-rooted respect for those who have fruitful ministries and those who demonstrate God's call and backing. Specifically, those who live in Latin America feel that it is an honor and privilege to serve those who are in spiritual authority over them. Somehow, they know that when they bless and serve those who serve the Lord, they will reap a much greater benefit—the favor of God.

Generally speaking, the last several hundred years of world history have seen many wars between many nations. There have been civil wars, two world wars, and a war on terror that has affected twenty percent of the globe, lasting over a decade. At the core of the human heart is a tendency to rebel against authority. Both world wars started in Europe, as did fascism, Marxism, and communism. These countries (the United States included), which are supposedly the most advanced and developed, have seen the greatest levels of political, social, and religious turmoil in the last five hundred years. The lack of respect for authority found in Euro-American culture is high compared to areas in Latin America, Asia, and Africa where revival is spreading.

The United States, for example, was born out of a rebellion over taxes. The amount was minimal, but it was enough to go to war, killing more than eighty thousand on both sides. Today, people distrust their governor, president, congressperson, and just about everyone in politics. I dare not ask what your opinion is of the President of the United States, your senator, congressional representative, governor, or mayor.

Our culture tends to disrespect those in local authority. When a highway patrol officer pulls us over, for example, two things usually go through our minds: *He probably has a quota to fill*. Or, *Why don't these guys spend their time chasing real criminals?*

Unfortunately, these rebellious tendencies affect the way we view leadership in churches, synagogues, and many other faith-based movements. In the countries where there are hardly any miracles, people generally do not respect their pastoral leadership. When people talk about their pastor, they refer to him as one of the guys. We scrutinize his sermons. We hold him (and his family) to a higher standard, but we don't show him a sliver of the same respect and honor as pastors are given in countries where miracles are prevalent.

Showing Honor and Respect for Spiritual Authority

As Jesus was ramping up his preaching ministry, he sent out seventy-two disciples to prepare the way. He told them not to take any supplies for their journey. He instructed them to stay only in one house and only where they were welcomed. When they entered a town, they were to eat what was set before them. Then he told them to heal the sick and proclaim, "The kingdom of God is near you" (Luke 10:9). However, if they were not welcomed, they were to go into the streets and shake the dust of the town off their feet. Jesus went on to say, "I tell you, it will be more bearable on that day for Sodom than for that town . . . He who listens to you listens to me; he who rejects you rejects me; but he who rejects me rejects him who sent me" (Luke 10:12–16).

These are strong words for people who do not honor those who are in spiritual authority, those who have been sent by the Lord to do God's will. Jesus equates disrespect and the judgment it brings to what Sodom endured when it was wiped from the face of the earth.

Several verses later (v. 17), the disciples return from the journey rejoicing. They say, "Lord, even the demons submit to us in your name." This could only mean one thing. People were healed. They were delivered from demonic oppression. Towns were transformed by the power of God. In essence, miracles happened, because the disciples were welcomed and accepted by the people in those towns. They were honored, respected, and appreciated. People opened their homes to them, fed them, and provided for their needs. The people accepted the message that the Kingdom of God was at hand.

Several years ago, I had a conversation with a friend who pastors a large church in Argentina. Claudio Friedzon is the pastor of King of Kings in Buenos Aires. He told me that before the revival started in Argentina in the 1980s, pastoral meetings were cold and fruitless. Pastors spent time complaining about their denominational leadership and then would conclude their meeting with a short time of prayer without any passion or faith. The meetings were poorly attended. He went on to say that after the revival hit Argentina, the pastors experienced a significant transformation. One of the first things that disappeared was their lack of respect for authority. Competition and pride began to dissipate as they held their leadership in greater esteem. The repercussions of the revival in Argentina have literally impacted the entire globe. One of the most prominent characteristics of the revival is how Argentine pastors have a genuine sense of humility, which directly contradicts the pride for which Argentines are famous. If revival turned their pride on its ear, you can imagine what revival would do to our arrogant American church culture.

You may ask what honor and respect for spiritual authority have to do with faith and miracles? There is a strong biblical example for the connection. In Luke 7:1–10, there is a beautiful story about one man's faith. I've studied this passage in college and have heard wonderful lectures about the centurion whose servant had fallen ill. Recently, though, I discovered an interesting correlation that Jesus makes between faith and respect for authority. He equates the two in this context.

Jesus entered a town called Capernaum about twenty miles from Nazareth. A centurion was deeply concerned about his servant who was about to die. He heard about the miracles that Jesus did and the spiritual authority he had. So the centurion pleaded with some of the elders of the Jews to ask Jesus to go and heal his servant. This first dispatch was made up of officials who had authority but were not necessarily people whom the centurion trusted unconditionally. When they went to Jesus, their negotiations were effective. They said, "This man deserves to have you do this, because he loves our nation and has built our synagogue" (v. 5). I'm not sure if Jesus was a fundraiser, but he obviously appreciated those who invested their finances so that God's Word would be proclaimed. So Jesus went with them.

When the entourage gets close to the house, the centurion has a change of heart of sorts. He realizes whom he is asking and what he is asking of him. So he decides to send a second group made up of personal friends. The centurion's respect comes through in the message that he sends to Jesus with his personal confidants: "Lord, don't trouble yourself, for I do not deserve to have you come under my roof" (v. 6). The centurion makes it clear that he is not worthy to have such a holy, powerful, and godly man come into his home. He goes on to say, "That is why I did not even consider myself worthy to come to you. But say the word, and my servant will be healed" (v. 7). Here he publically proclaims that Jesus has the authority to send a word of healing to the ill servant. Suddenly, the story takes on a whole new nuance as the centurion states his understanding of the spiritual pecking order. In essence, the centurion implies that he can see what most people in Israel cannot see. He says, "For I myself am a man under authority, with soldiers under me. I tell this one, 'Go,' and he goes; and that one, 'Come,' and he comes. I say to my servant, 'Do this,' and he does it" (v. 8).

To this, Jesus says nothing about the centurion's wonderful depiction of respect and authority. He does not say, "I have not seen such great respect for authority." Instead, he turns to the crowd and says, "I tell you, I have not found such great faith even in Israel" (v. 9). Jesus equates the centurion's respect for Jesus' power and authority with having great faith.

As believers, we cannot discount any passage where Jesus uses such powerful language. The centurion's humility and recognition of spiritual authority moves the hand of God and brings healing to his servant. The centurion, a man with authority and under authority bows to a greater authority. That respect moved the hand of God. His faith, in this sense, is so great that Jesus doesn't need to take one step closer to the house. It is no surprise to the readers of Luke's Gospel that when the centurion's friends returned to the house, they found the servant well.

Frequent Flyers vs. Flight Attendants

In churches and parachurch organizations around the world, we have two types of people who attend or participate on a regular basis. I call them *flight attendants* and *frequent fliers*. Frequent flyers know when a flight is smooth. They can tell if the weather is clear or cloudy. Provided it's a clear day, they can tell which direction the plane is flying. They cannot fly the plane, however. They may think they can, but they are indeed incapable. Flight attendants, on the other hand, can do the same things that frequent flyers can, but they exist to serve. They exist first and foremost to assist the captain and flight crew, then secondly the passengers. In case of an emergency, some crewmembers are trained to handle problems in the cockpit and main cabin.

In all my years of flying (over a half a million miles), I've never heard a flight attendant talk bad about a pilot, especially the pilot who was flying the plane. Frequent fliers complain about the seats, the service, the flight, the turbulence, temperature, entertainment, and some might even offer suggestions on how to fly. Further, I have never seen another pilot sitting in the main cabin looking out the window saying, "Where in the world is this guy flying?" Or, "Did you hear that noise? Something must be wrong! Boy if I were flying this plane, I'd be heading in an entirely different direction."

In the same way, the church is made up of frequent flyers and flight attendants. The frequent flyers show up once a week and tell the pastor and staff everything they're doing wrong and everything that needs to change. They regularly undermine the staff's spiritual leadership by talking behind their backs, looking for a way to change the church into what they think it should become. They may think they know how to pastor a church, but just like the frequent flyer, they cannot. Instead, they should try to become like a flight attendant and resist the spirit of mutiny. In the same way a flight attendant comes with an attitude to serve and assist the pilot, so should those of us who attend local churches. We should seek to serve instead of thinking that we know how to fly the plane. Think about it this way, if we wouldn't tolerate insubordination in the armed forces, why would we think that the Lord would allow it in the Kingdom of God?

Christians in Latin America, Asia, and Africa have a significant amount of respect for their pastors and leadership. They esteem them. They honor them. They value them greatly. And in those parts of the world there is a higher frequency of healings, miracles, and revival. If we want to see an outbreak of miracles, healings, and revival across our land, we must rid ourselves of spiritual arrogance and pride and show respect to those God has placed as a spiritual authority over us. Until this happens, we will never see the breakthroughs we yearn to see.

I'm quite sure that the people in Nazareth wanted to see miracles. Yet it was their lack of respect that prevented them from experiencing the power of God. When Jesus first arrived in his hometown, people marveled at his teaching. They were impressed with his wisdom and went so far as to admit that he could do miracles. Then for some reason they looked for a way to lower Jesus to their level. They asked, "'Isn't this the carpenter? Isn't this Mary's son and the brother of James, Joseph, Judas, and Simon? Aren't his sisters here with us?' And they took offense at him" (Mark 6:3). People become offended when one of their own rises to stardom. Humans often enjoy watching a superstar humbled. That's when Jesus made that famous statement, "Only in his hometown, among his relatives and in his own house is a prophet without honor" (Mark 6:4).

According to verse five of Mark 6, Jesus could only do a few miracles in his hometown because of their lack of faith, which was manifested in their lack of respect for his authority. Mentioning his family, his upbringing, and his occupation was an attempt to humiliate Jesus, which is why he equated their lack of respect with lack of faith.

It is no coincidence that revivals all over the world ignite because of an eventual openness to the messenger and message. In Latin America, for example, four hundred people are coming to the know Christ every hour of every day, every week, every month, every year, twenty-four hours a day. In 1900, there were fifty thousand evangelicals in Latin America. Today, there are over 120 million, and eighty-five percent are Spirit-filled and pray with the expectancy of receiving miracles on a regular basis. Missionaries carried the message of good news on horseback, mule, in canoes, into the cities of Mexico, throughout the regions of rain forest of Central America, and into the deepest parts of the Amazon jungle. The result of their efforts has been unprecedented. Latin Americans are the most receptive people group to the Gospel of Jesus Christ in the history of the world. Why? In the places of Latin America where revival is prevalent, they accept the messenger and message with open arms and do so with great respect.

If you are a leader and don't see miracles happening in your life or ministry, maybe there's a lack of respect and honor in your midst. Perhaps those you lead need to learn to show honor and respect. Or, perhaps, you do. We need to keep in mind that honor and respect flows in two directions—to us and from us. Like being a servant, showing someone how to honor and respect is best taught by modeling. The most effective way to teach these concepts to those who follow is to demonstrate that we are honoring and respecting those in spiritual authority in our lives.

What Comes Around, Goes Around

Why is this so important? This chapter centers on the concept of *we reap what we sow*. Recently, I spoke to a school district in Ohio. I gave a keynote speech to educators about their need to respect their principals, district board, and officials. The look on their faces said it all. They were not thrilled about hearing the importance of submitting to authority.

I asked them, "How many of you remember being in elementary school?" Nearly all of them raised their hands. Then I asked, "How many of you feel that there was a higher degree of respect for your teacher when you went to school then what your students show you in the classroom today?" Again, nearly all of them raised their hands. "How many of you say that the students who are the most disrespectful advance the least?" Again, most of the hands went up.

Then I said, "Unless someone teaches your students the importance of showing honor and respect, they will grow up to be disrespectful and dishonorable adults. This is a vicious cycle that must be broken. So if parents don't model the concept of respecting authority to their children, you as teachers must do so by showing respect to those who you serve." That's when the light went on in their minds. Showing honor and respect in the classroom opens the door for scholastic advancement. In the same way, showing honor and respect to those who lead us spiritually opens the door to the favor of God. Ultimately, we reap what we sow.

Four Ways for Leaders to Earn Respect

Everyone is a leader, and everyone is a follower. What determines whether we lead of follow are the people around us at that given moment. There are four things leaders can do to cultivate the respect and honor necessary to experience miracles in their midst. First, a leader must become a person *worthy of respect and honor.* Respect and honor cannot be demanded. They must be earned, and people will only respect and honor someone they *trust*.

Do those who God is calling you to lead find it easy to trust you? Do they believe that you have their best interests in mind when you make decisions that affect them? If not, you must treat every decision that affects them as if it were your last one and one that contributes to your legacy. As one of my mentors, Zig Ziglar, has said on many occasions, "You can have anything in life you want as long as you're willing to help enough other people get what they want."[1]

Second, those who follow you must *feel accepted and welcomed*. Latin Americans, Asians, and Africans in ministry find it much easier to respect and accept others in ministry. They reach across denominational lines much easier than we Westerners do. In your context, remember that followers should not feel discriminated against, belittled, or less valuable than others. The affluent shouldn't be treated with greater respect than the homeless. In the Kingdom of God there are no favorites, and there should never be any competition. As Paul says,

> The eye cannot say to the hand, "I don't need you!" And the head cannot say to the feet, "I don't need you!" On the contrary, those parts of the body that seem to be

> weaker are indispensable, and the parts that we think are less honorable we treat with special honor. And the parts that are unpresentable are treated with special modesty, while our presentable parts need no special treatment. But God has combined the members of the body and has given greater honor to the parts that lacked it, so that there should be no division in the body, but that its parts should have equal concern for each other. If one part suffers, every part suffers with it; if one part is honored, every part rejoices with it. (1 Cor. 12:21–26)

Third, your *commitment to the cause and ministerial mission must be apparent*. Do your followers see that you are more than willing to make a significant sacrifice for the cause? If you are not willing to lay down your personal criteria for the mission, you cannot expect anyone else to do so either. The disciples only became willing to lay down their lives after seeing what Jesus did on the cross. Once they saw that he was committed to the salvation of the world, they became willing to lay down their lives as well.

Fourth, spiritual leaders must demonstrate that they are *backed by the Great I Am*. This is perhaps the most important element that calls people to respect and honor you as a leader. There is one comment that members of our crusade team have said to me that stands out more than anything else. They say, "God's backing is evident every night of every crusade and in every altar call." Nothing gives a spiritual leader more credibility than this. Ultimately, it is the Lord who delegates authority, but we must use that authority in the areas where he has granted us permission to use it.

One of the reasons people in the United States and different parts of Europe do not respect those in ministry is that many ministers do not exercise the authority that Christ has given them. They have become spiritual pacifists. They do not engage the enemy when attacked, and many times fail to recognize that spiritual forces are waging war against them. In addition, many ministers consistently use the phrase, "Whatever God's will is." Or when they pray, they say, "If it's your will." They don't use these phrases with humility but rather as an excuse, because they do not know the will of God. Not only do the principalities of darkness enjoy battling against fireless, passionless, and powerless ministers, but lay people find it frustrating to follow spiritual leaders who lack power and authority. In the same way that passengers want to believe that their pilot has an idea where he is flying the plane, people in churches need to sense that their spiritual leaders have an understanding of God's will and that they will use their spiritual authority to work toward bringing about his will on earth as it is in heaven.

So if you are a leader, I challenge you to use your spiritual authority and demonstrate that God backs you. The fact that God has called you must be evident to those who follow you. Using your spiritual authority properly will bring about the respect you need from those who follow you.

King David is considered one of the greatest leaders in history. Did his followers trust him? Did they believe that he had their best interests in mind when he made decisions regarding the kingdom? Absolutely. He also treated people with respect, especially those in authority over him. David's commitment to the call of God, the direction of Israel, and the importance of worshiping only the Lord was apparent to every one of his followers. It was clear to those who followed him that David would have laid down his life for the cause. The story of his battle with Goliath clearly demonstrates this.

Could David's followers easily see that he had God's backing? Yes! Even Jonathan, King Saul's son, loved and respected David. He recognized that David was so trustworthy that the Lord picked him, not Jonathan, to follow Saul as king (1 Sam. 23:17). On more than one occasion Jonathan swore his allegiance to David.

Let me add a final thought regarding David's leadership. Many times when King Saul tried to kill him, David refused to retaliate. Instead he said, "But the LORD forbid that I should lay a hand on the LORD'S anointed" (1 Sam. 26:11). Even though David was anointed king, he refused to show any disrespect or speak ill of his predecessor. His life serves as a great example to every leader who struggles with conflicts with a predecessor.

All in all, a spiritual leader must be worthy of respect. A true leader doesn't command people to follow. A true leader is someone that people want to follow. That is the individual to whom people will graciously show honor and respect.

Four Ways to Show Honor and Respect

If you desire to experience miracles and God's favor, you must break the habit of being disrespectful, dissentious, and negative and instead develop a servant's heart. You begin this process by self-checking your attitude. Make it a point not to participate in the wrong kind of gossip or in undermining conversations. If you struggle with bitterness, choose to forgive and move on. Forgiveness is not an emotion. It's a choice, just like the decision to not gossip. Once you've checked your own heart, begin to focus on the following four areas where you can show honor and respect to those you serve.

First, *aim to serve* without any recognition or strings attached. Every time we see Andrew in the New Testament, he is bringing someone to Jesus. He is not part of the negative dialogue. He doesn't complain about the impossible situation in which he finds himself. Instead, he works behind the scenes to solve a problem for his Master. When Jesus told the disciples to feed the five thousand, they complained about not having enough resources. Andrew, on the other hand, brought to Jesus a boy who had some bread and fish. He wasn't looking for credit. He simply wanted to be a part of the solution. When your leader needs solutions, work diligently to help find them. Jump in with both feet to be what Jesus values most in the Kingdom, a servant.

In Latin America, Africa, and Asia, Christians serve and serve and serve. When they are done serving, they serve even more. They use their vacation time to serve. They use their homes to serve. Many times they'll invest their own resources to enhance their ministry of service. They do not look for compensation or a special place at the table for their service, and they would never consider it a sacrifice. To them, it's an honor to serve.

Second, *reach out to your leaders personally,* at least, where the relationship permits you to do so. Look for ways to serve them. Look for ways to honor them. Remember, what we feel is honorable may not be honorable to them. Everyone is different, so research, ask, and discover what your leaders feel best helps and blesses them.

Jesus gave us a hint of what honors him greatly. He asked Peter three times, "Do you love me?" "Of course, I love you," Peter replied. "Feed my lambs, and feed my sheep," the Lord said. Peter dedicated his life to preaching the Gospel and taking care of the followers of Christ. He honored the Lord with his life. When we take care of each other, we honor the Lord. So inquire and find out what specifically honors the leaders that God has put in your life.

Third, *be a finder of the good*. Look for the good in the spiritual leaders in your life. Negative attitudes never cultivate miracles, and they hardly produce positive results. I've never seen a pessimist receive a miracle, and even if something miraculous happens, they quickly downplay it or dismiss it. Talk positively about the ministry in which you are involved and about the leaders who serve you. Look for ways that demonstrate your true appreciation for them. The point is that when people see you, they get a sense that you esteem your leadership, church, or parachurch organization.

Fourth, *pray for your leaders*. We need to realize that as soon as someone decides to do something for God, that person has a bullseye on his or her back. The Lord has commissioned them into a war over the souls of everyone on the planet. It's a war against the rulers, authorities, and the principalities of darkness, against the spiritual forces of evil in the heavenly realms, according to Ephesians 6:12.

Honoring those in spiritual authority over us is one of the characteristics of godly faith. At the same time, there are instances when God sees our lack of respect and equates that with a lack of faith. Many times when we don't respect the people God has put in our lives, miracles simply do not happen.

When we need a miracle and nothing happens, we often ask ourselves, do I have enough faith? Perhaps the more appropriate question in light of what we studied in this chapter is, do I show honor and respect to my spiritual authority and most importantly to the Lord? Or, do I undermine others with my attitudes, words, or deeds? Am I like the centurion who clearly saw the spiritual pecking order, or am I having difficulty making the connection between faith and honor?

The good news is that change is possible, and it's never too late. Friend, from the depths of my heart, I want to convey to you, *become what you believe!*

The following prayer is a starting point for you. I believe that God will help you become someone of great faith as we have outlined it in this chapter.

> *Father, help me respect and honor those you have placed in my life. Give me the heart of a true servant, because I know that's what you want me to have. Whenever my attitude impedes your hand from doing miracles, please show me what I need to do to find favor in your eyes.*
>
> *Help me to find favor in the eyes of those I serve, both as a leader and a follower. Help me to become the member of the body of Christ you've destined me to become. Show me your will, your powerful hand at work, and your miracle-working power. I want to experience the miraculous. In Christ's name. Amen.*

Questions for discussion or personal reflection

1. In what ways does the idea of submitting to authority not set well with you? As you read this chapter, what leader has God brought to mind as someone you need to forgive? Which leader in your life do you need to make more of an effort to respect?

2. In what ways have you been less than honorable toward your governmental leaders, occupational leaders, and spiritual leaders?

3. Who in your life has a healthy balance of showing respect yet not being a blind disciple?

Chapter Five
THE PROCESS OF A MIRACLE

Angelina was escorted into the tent just before the evangelistic meeting started. Years earlier, she had contracted an incurable disease that destroyed her optic nerve. The sixty-year-old Paraguayan was completely blind.

Richard and Janice Larson were missionaries launching a church plant in Asunción and were part of a task force assigned to Paraguay. The services they led that night were televised. In addition to the large tent and sound system, they had rigged several 1,500-watt quartz lights to illuminate the stage for the cameras.

At the end of the evening, Richard asked the people if anyone needed physical healing. Many people raised their hands, including Angelina. He asked each one what their issues were, as was his custom. When he came to Angelina, she told him that she was blind and was asking God to restore her sight.

"Can you see anything?" he asked.

"Nothing," she replied.

Richard waved his hands in front of her eyes with her head facing toward the quartz lights, which produced a significant amount of heat. The television lights combined with the Paraguayan summer heat made standing on the stage nearly unbearable. The only thing Angelina sensed was a noticeable change in temperature on her face as his hands passed in front of the blazing lights. Richard and Angelina prayed, and afterward, she said, "I'll come back tomorrow."

Angelina returned every night for a week, and each night Richard asked if there was any change in her condition. She said no. Then they prayed. A week later, she pointed in the direction of the overhead projector. Angelina said, "I see something that looks shiny." She was gesturing toward something underneath the projector fan. The quartz lights were reflecting off of the chrome legs that held the projector. It was the first time in years that her optic nerve registered something. Upon hearing this, the crowd erupted into applause.

After a week, Angelina noticed more bright images, including Richard's white tie. One night she said, "I see something that looks like a bump or package." It was Richard's face. He replied, "Well, eventually you will see that what you're looking at is not the most beautiful face in Paraguay." Everyone laughed.

As the weeks passed, Angelina's eyesight steadily improved. People faithfully attended with anticipation of what God would do in their lives, but there were some who paid close attention to what would happen with Angelina. Her slow-motion healing created anticipation, expectation, and most importantly hope in the hearts of those in attendance. God's healing was working at a pace that allowed many people to witness it firsthand.

After a month, Richard Larson asked Angelina to do something she hadn't been able to do in years. He invited her on stage to read a portion of the Bible. It was a large-print version, but considering she was in her sixties, that wasn't unusual. As she read the scripture that night, everyone in the campaign saw the completion of a miracle that changed Angelina's life for the glory of God.

As we continue our journey of discovering New Testament faith, this chapter deals with the fifth characteristic found in those who experience the miraculous. In contrast to what most Western Europeans and North Americans tend to believe regarding the immediacy of the miraculous, Christians in Latin America, Africa, and Asia believe that *miracles can happen through a process*. For them, a miracle may take seconds, days, weeks, or even months. Much like those who lived in the New Testament, those who experience miracles in other parts of the world do not hold God to a time limit.

Miracles Can Happen Over Time

As I researched the fifty-two miracles found in the four Gospels, I looked for patterns. When a story doesn't follow a common thread or developing theme, it stands out. One of the most peculiar stories in the New Testament is found in Mark 8:22–26. As Jesus arrives at the small town of Bethsaida, several people bring a blind man to him. They beg Jesus to lay hands on the man so that he will be healed. Without saying a word, Jesus takes the man by the hand and leads him outside the city. Then he spits on the man's eyes and places his hands on him. From this point forward, three things happen that are not seen anywhere else in the New Testament.

First, Jesus asks the man, "Do you see anything?" (v. 23). Mark doesn't tell us why Jesus asks the question. Perhaps the lack of an immediate response prompts the Lord to break the awkward silence. For a brief moment it seems unclear if the man has received healing. This is the only time in the New Testament that Jesus lays hands on someone and that person is not immediately healed.

The man gazes up and answers, "I see people; they look like trees walking around" (v. 24). He obviously was able to see at one point in his life. Otherwise, he would not have a reference for people or trees.

Jesus once again lays hands on him, and the man experiences total and complete healing. This is the second unique quality in this story. Aside from this episode in the New Testament, Christ never has to make a second effort in order for someone to receive healing.

Third, the Lord directs the man to go home with the explicit instruction, "Don't go into the village" (v. 26). In other New Testament stories, the Lord tells people not to say anything after they receive healing. Sometimes, he directs them to show themselves to the priests and religious leaders as a testimony of the power of God. Sometimes, Jesus tells them to proclaim the great things God has done to the people where they live. He never tells people to avoid towns or villages. In this case, though, Jesus explicitly tells the man not to go into the village, which strongly suggests that there is something about the town that was not suitable for the man. Mark doesn't elaborate, but the development of the story makes it clear. Jesus leads the man out of the town so that he can perform the miracle, then tells him not to go back into the town. This third characteristic is key for us to understand what may hinder God's miracle-working power in our lives.

Sometimes, our surroundings cause an emotional sickness or even a physical one. Perhaps the people with whom we interact produce in us bad attitudes, discouragement, or even lack of faith. Some people simply bring out the worst in us.

In many ways, we are like the blind man. There are moments when God wants to take us by the hand and separate us from the rest of the crowd, where he can be one-on-one with us. He wants to do the miraculous. He wants to set the captive free and bind up the brokenhearted. However, the competing ideas in our head drown out the comprehensible direction of

God. The faithless influences detract us from fully understanding God's plan. So the Lord sovereignly steps into our lives and removes us from our context.

All of these insights bring us to one of the central lessons in the story of the blind man from Bethsaida. God sticks with us until his work is complete. Whether his work takes place through a process or happens immediately, God is faithful to finish the good work that he starts in us (1 Thess. 5:24, Phil. 1:6). He will remove us, change our circumstances, and do what is necessary to implement his perfect and pleasing will. And many times, his instructions to us are don't go back to your old life.

Among the many lessons we learn from Mark 8:22–26 is that God cannot be put into a box. By that, I mean that the Lord does what he wants, when he wants, and how he wants. There are no formulas when it comes to when, how, and to what degree God chooses to intervene.

From time to time people ask me, "Didn't Jesus have enough power to heal the man even while they were in the town? Couldn't he have healed him the first time? Wouldn't God's healing stick with the man whether or not he returned to the town?" There is no doubt that God had the power to make the necessary adjustments, but he didn't. Why? Most likely, the man's faith was still being established. He was still learning to trust the Lord. More often than not, God's intervention works through our faith. It's true that there are a few occasions in the Bible when God demonstrates his power without any faith on our behalf. In most cases, however, Jesus says it is our faith that moves God to overcome the laws of nature, the clutches of the demonic, and the crippling affects of disease to bring us to a place of restoration.

Let me ask you, are you looking for a miracle? Do you need a breakthrough? If so, does God need to remove you from your circumstances? Are you in a place where the influences dilute or derail your faith? Is your world damaging or unsuitable for your spiritual well-being? Think about it for a moment. Is there something that God must remove from your life in order for you to experience his powerful breakthrough?

Having the Eyes to See Miracles in Slow Motion

Believers in Latin America, Africa, and Asia understand that a miracle can come immediately or over time. They view their lives moving in the direction of redemption, deliverance, and healing in every area. As I mentioned in chapter 3, people in these cultures value time differently than we do. So they do not see any conflict in asking God each day for the same miracle, while believing that God is guiding them through the process. For them, the progress might be slow, but it's still moving. For that reason, people like Angelina will make the extraordinary effort to attend every night of an evangelistic campaign that lasts several months.

The Western European and North American mindset cannot fathom attending a healing campaign every night for two months. First, we don't have the patience, we don't have the time, and we have too many other *important* things to do.

Second, we are a culture that personifies the notion of *I want it now.* If we have to wait for it, make an extraordinary effort to attain it, or walk a distance to get it, then it's not worth it. There are thousands of fast-food restaurants scattered across North America and Western Europe. Why? Because we want our food in less than sixty seconds. According to Apple, there are over

1 million apps available for the iOS platform alone. Each one is designed to meet a need (or entertain us) faster than doing things in a conventional way, and every one of them can be downloaded in a matter of seconds from just about anywhere in the world. The benefit to *our fast paced, easy to get it* lifestyle is that what once took us days or even weeks to accomplish, we can now do in minutes. The drawback is that we are becoming people who have no patience to wait for anything, much less to wait on God.

In contrast, those who live in other parts of the world don't have a problem standing in line for church or waiting on God for days, months, or even years. They do not have a problem seeing miracles in slow motion.

Third, the Euro-American mindset finds it difficult to interpret slow-motion miracles. If we pray at an altar for something that would be obvious (physical healing, for example), and the miracle doesn't happen immediately, then we believe our prayers are not answered. If God doesn't move now, heal now, or deliver now, than it's time to move on and figure out another way to solve our problem.

Recently, I interviewed my good friend Alex on my radio program. He lives in Cuba and was traveling in the United States visiting several churches. I asked him to share a story on the air of someone in his country who God touched miraculously. He said, "A couple of years ago, a pastor's daughter was diagnosed with a rare form of leukemia. The four-year-old girl grew worse with each passing day. They used the best forms of chemotherapy, yet instead of getting better, she grew worse. After seven long months, the doctors gave up and stopped treatment. They called a meeting with the girl's parents and explained everything they had done and how in spite of the best medical treatments, the girl's body did not respond. They somberly told her parents that she would pass away within two weeks."

I could tell that Alex felt overwhelmed as he described the discussion between the doctors and the parents. He paused for a brief moment and then continued. "I remember praying with her parents several times a week. I remember crying with them as well. We asked every person and every pastor we knew to join us in prayer. Then when all medical hope was lost, something miraculous happened. When she was what seemed to be only a few days away from death, suddenly her blood count showed signs of improvement. Within ten days, she was completely healed."

I asked him what the doctors thought of her recovery. He said, "Two of her doctors couldn't believe it. They were self-proclaimed atheists who felt that we were filled with false hope and denial. So they ordered test after test, because they were convinced that her condition would worsen at any given moment. They ordered one test a week, but when her tests returned negative, they slowed the frequency to once a month. Then they ordered them once a quarter; then once every six months; and finally, once a year. Eight years ago, they finally declared her leukemia-free. Since that time, she has been perfectly healthy."

I asked him how long it was from the time that she was diagnosed until the time she received her healing. He said, "Seven months." I asked him at what time did God's miracle start. He replied, "Weeks before anyone ever knew it."

Those who have the faith to see the power of God have no problem seeing miracles as a process that may take hours, days, weeks, months, or even years. They have the eyes to see miracles in slow motion. They would tell you that no one can put a sovereign God in a box. They serve as a good model for us in this sense. If we are willing to relearn and be re-discipled, I believe that regardless of who we are or where we live, we too can have the faith that moves the hand of God. We can experience God's miracle-working power right where we are.

Expecting Miracles in God's Timing

Recently, I shared in a worship service the story from chapter 2 of this book of the little girl who was miraculously healed of curvature of the spine. When the service ended, a woman named Judy walked up to me with tears in her eyes. She asked me if I would pray for her. I knew beyond the shadow of a doubt that as I asked her the question, do you believe God can do this? her answer would be an unwavering yes. At the time, the seventy-four-year-old was facing stage-four breast cancer. Judy had been in a battle for fourteen long years.

Every time she saw her oncologist, Judy reminded her that God was at work in her body and people were praying for her recovery. The doctor seemed indifferent.

After Judy and I prayed, I felt that God would honor her faith. There was something in her eyes that conveyed a spiritual confidence. Over the course of a year, she showed signs of improvement, but in March of the following year, something miraculous took place. Her blood tests showed a significant improvement. Her doctor prescribed a new chemotherapy pill and said that she wouldn't notice any difference for at least two months. Within a month, Judy experienced such a significant change that her cancer indicators fell below normal. Her oncologist was shocked.

Her doctor entered the examining room with wide eyes and

stated that she had never seen anything like it. Judy then asked her oncologist if she could see how God answers prayer and how he was working in her body. Her oncologist agreed wholeheartedly. In Judy's mind, God uses every means available to bring healing to her body. In the end, God always has the last word. Judy also has learned to expect miracles in God's timing.

At what point exactly did God's miracle-working power begin to heal Judy's body? No one really knows. One thing is certain, though. Everyone, including Judy's oncologist, can see something extraordinary about her recovery that cannot be explained by science. Everyone agrees that something miraculous took place.

Judy doesn't live in Africa, Latin America, or Asia. She lives in Southern California. She doesn't live in poverty. She doesn't have a degree in theology or have many resources at her disposal. She simply believes. She takes God at his word, and she is willing to trust him. Her testimony demonstrates that anyone anywhere at any time can experience God's power. The key lesson in this chapter is to understand that miracles come in God's timing, not ours.

There's a wonderful story in the New Testament that illustrates this point. In Luke 17, Jesus is heading into a village when ten lepers call out to him from a distance, "Jesus, Master, have pity on us" (v. 13). He takes a good look at them and replies, "Go, show yourselves to the priests" (v.14). Then Luke writes, "And as they went, they were cleansed" (v. 14). One of the problems with the English language is that it doesn't have two past tenses like other languages. It's hard for us to describe an ongoing process over time. Other languages have verb conjugations to describe past process with greater accuracy. So a more precise way of describing what Luke writes (which is how it reads in Spanish as well) would be, "During the time that the lepers were heading from the place where they met Jesus until they reached the priests, their bodies were healed."

I imagine that there was reason to celebrate, and perhaps the recipients of the miracle were a bit distracted. After all, a miracle of that magnitude would change your life forever. But the story doesn't end there. Luke goes on to describe something that is crucial in God's eyes. "One of them, when he saw he was healed, came back, praising God in a loud voice. He threw himself at Jesus' feet and thanked him—and he was a Samaritan" (Luke 17:15–16). Not only does Luke point out that the man was not a Jew, but that he was the only one that came back and thanked Jesus. Imagine that. Only one out of ten came back, and he was a foreigner. That is surprising. Apparently, Jesus was surprised as well. He goes on to finish the story with a familiar phrase, "Rise and go; your faith has made you well" (v. 19).

This is a powerful lesson for readers of this book. Be grateful to God. If you receive a miracle, give God thanks. Show your appreciation. We must be careful not to become like those who experience wonderful things in life but are never content. For some, it's never good enough. Guard your heart, and show your appreciation for the life God has given you. Remember, God is always watching to see how we will react; to see how truly grateful we are.

Setbacks, Detours, and Seeming Defeats

I know people who have been waiting for a miracle for decades, and to be transparent, I'm one of them. I run two to three miles a day. I eat between 1,700 and 1,900 calories a day. I avoid red meat, eliminate saturated fats, and minimize my intake of sodium. Still, my cholesterol and blood pressure without strong medication would be at critical levels. I have a genetic problem that has no permanent solution aside from pharmaceutical drugs. I read, study, pray, fast, and ask others to pray for me. It seems as though I'm stuck in a holding pattern. And I know that's the way thousands upon thousands of other people feel.

On our road to deliverance, healing, and restoration, we face setbacks. We're forced to take detours. Many times, we sit with our head in our hands feeling an overwhelming sense of defeat. Shadrach, Meshach, and Abednego faced an impossible situation. They knew that God forbade them to bow down to false idols. So when King Nebuchadnezzar made a ninety-foot idol and commanded everyone in the kingdom to bow down and worship it or be thrown into the blazing furnace, I'm sure they felt overwhelmed. As the trumpet blew and everyone bowed down and worshipped the statue, they didn't. When the king heard about it, he was furious. He ordered them to explain why they refused to obey his law.

Knowing that the fiery furnace awaited them, Shadrach, Meshach, and Abednego could have buckled under pressure. Instead, they were resolute and showed great faith. Their response portrays the attitude of many people living in places where revival is prevalent and miracles are frequent. They said,

> "O Nebuchadnezzar, we do not need to defend ourselves before you in this matter. If we are thrown into the blazing furnace, the God we serve is able to save us from it, and he will rescue us from your hand, O king. But even if he does not, we want you to know, O king, that we will not serve your gods or worship the image of gold you

have set up." (Dan. 3:16–18)

That determination is what true faith is all about. It's not based on feelings. It's not grounded in false hopes. It's founded on an absolute trust that your life is ultimately in God's hands. It's the notion that says even if my God doesn't deliver me, I will continue to believe and stand with him.

Filled with rage, Nebuchadnezzar ordered the furnace heated seven times hotter than usual. He had the three men tied and thrown in. It was so hot that the flames killed the soldiers who threw Shadrach, Meshach, and Abednego into the furnace. Suddenly, something miraculous took place. The king was the first to notice it. He turned to his advisers and asked, "'Weren't there three men that we tied up and threw into the fire?' They replied, 'Certainly, O king.' He said, 'Look! I see four men walking around in the fire, unbound and unharmed, and the fourth looks like a son of the gods.'" The king saw that the Lord had indeed saved Shadrach, Meshach, and Abednego, so he released them from the furnace.

The story ended well, but not all do. Such was the life of a personal friend of mine who died of cancer. He believed that God was going to heal him until his dying breath. The Apostle Paul prayed three times for his thorn in the flesh to be removed, but God said that his grace was sufficient. I am quite sure that the disciples looked for God's deliverance from persecution and martyrdom. You see, part of the price of New Testament faith is being willing to stand with Christ regardless of the outcome. That's the point of being a true disciple, which is why I am convinced that Christians in Africa, Latin America, and Asia see more miracles and are much more willing to count the cost of discipleship then many of us in North America and

Western Europe.

I want to leave you with a final challenge in this chapter. Be resolute. Be determined. Come what may, make sure your commitment to God is unfailing and unwavering. Stand with Shadrach, Meshach, and Abednego and say, "Even if my God doesn't deliver me, I will not cave in to doubt or unbelief. I will not bow down to any false god just to save my life." Know that if you are a disciple of Christ, your life is ultimately in his hands. You can rest assured that Christ has you moving (quickly or slowly) in his process regardless of where it may lead. God wants you to *become what you believe*.

I have written a prayer that I believe will help you connect with God during times of frustration, setback, or even defeat. If you are able, pray this prayer out loud and do so with a sincere heart. The Lord will guide you and help you.

Lord, it seems that for every step I take forward, I take two steps backward. Help me to see your mighty hand at work in my life. I need to see progress, and I need to see that you are truly guiding me. I know that I need to trust you more. So I pray for your peace to invade my life. I pray for your peace that passes all understanding.

During times of frustration, send me a word of encouragement. Whenever I feel that I am sliding, uphold me with your righteous right hand. Above all, regardless of the outcome, may you be glorified and may my life be a bright testimony of hope to others who need you during the darkest moments of their lives. I place my life in your hands and ask for your miracle to come in your timing. In Jesus' name. Amen.

Questions for discussion or personal reflection

1. Describe in a sentence or two something miraculous that you've seen in the last three to six months.

2. Was this miracle someone's deliverance from substance abuse, a supernatural intervention in your finances, or an unusual recovery from sickness? How long did it take for full recovery or restoration to take place? Was it instantaneous or over a period of time?

3. In what ways does this encourage your faith?

4. In light of the fact that many times God performs miracles through a process, how might this encourage you?

Chapter Six

Moving from Belief to Conviction

As we began the radio interview in the heart of Madrid's largest shopping mall, I asked Luis to describe how he came to Christ. The forty-two-year-old Spaniard wasn't raised in a religious home but did attend church somewhat regularly. Like most Europeans, his faith was cultural and traditional.

After moving from the country to the capital city of Madrid, Luis' sister contracted a sickness that infected the medulla or inner tissue brushing up against her spine. The doctors strongly recommended surgery to the girl's parents, but they had one major concern. "Any error in the operation could leave your daughter confined to a wheelchair for the rest of her life," the doctors said. When her parents heard those words, they were terrified.

The family was deeply concerned about the health of their daughter. About that time, their neighbors came by and mentioned that there was a circus tent in town, but it wasn't filled with animals or a trapeze. They said, "It is a campaign, and they've put out a huge sign that reads, 'Jesus is the healer of the body and soul.' We've gone a couple of times, and we found it to be very enlightening. You should go and see if there might be hope for your daughter." Luis and his family came from a traditional background like most families in Spain. They were not interested in going to another church meeting or listening to someone talk about religious things. They felt they had everything they needed.

As Luis told me their story he went on to say, "The God we knew was far and distant. We didn't have any sense that he could do anything in our circumstance. We would say good-bye to him when we left church and wouldn't see him until we returned to church the following Sunday. Frankly, we didn't have a personal relationship with him."

Despite the family's doubts, they decided to visit the tent because they needed a miracle. They noticed that the songs they heard there were about faith and the people were warm and friendly. Each night the speaker invited everyone to come forward after hearing the message. He asked the question, do you believe God can do a miracle in your life? Many people at the campaign verbally responded with the word *amen*. Luis and his family presented their petition for their daughter's healing before the Lord that night. Afterward, they went home. There was no outward evidence of an internal miracle and the family didn't think about it much in the days that followed. Instead, they headed to the southern coast of Spain for summer vacation. After a month, they returned to the capital, now faced with the reality that the date of the girl's surgery was approaching.

In the days leading up to the operation, the family took their daughter to the doctor's office to take x-rays. When the doctor read the results, he was in shock. The girl's vertebrae, spine, and all the surrounding tissue were clear of any infection or growth. The doctor asked, "What did you do?"

"Nothing," they replied.

"Where did you go," the doctor asked.

"We only went on vacation," they said.

Then the mother reflected upon the previous six weeks. She remembered the neighbor's invitation, going to the tent, and hearing a message about placing their faith in Christ. The pastor asked the question, *do you believe God can heal you?* and they chose to place their faith in God.

"God touched our daughter," she said. The entire family looked in amazement at each other as they realized what had happened. They continued to attend the evangelistic campaign faithfully. Today, Luis is the assistant pastor in Iglesia Nueva Vida in Madrid, Spain.

Many times we underestimate the importance of the question Jesus asks: Do you believe I can do this? It's a question that allows people to publicly verbalize their belief that Jesus is not only capable of performing the miraculous, but is willing to bring healing, restoration, deliverance, and salvation into our lives. It's a question that moves us from belief to conviction.

The sixth characteristic of those who experience the miraculous is a *willingness to publicly verbalize their faith in him before the miracle takes place*. Christians in Asia, Africa, and Latin America are more than willing to publicly verbalize their faith in Christ to perform a miracle even before they see any evidence of it. They reflect the same characteristic found in many recipients of miracles in the New Testament. It's a trait that is definitely missing in our cautious, non-committal Euro-American culture. The account of Jesus healing the two blind men (Matt. 9:27–31), which I briefly mentioned in the introduction, is what prompted me to write this book. It is worthwhile to look at the story again here.

After healing the daughter of a ruler, Jesus leaves the house and heads home. As soon as he walks out the door, two blind men begin following him. They raise their voices, begging him to take pity on them. "Mercy, Son of David! Mercy on us!", they cry. No one knows the distance between the ruler's house and Jesus' home. Still, Matthew makes it a point to state that the men continue to follow and plead with Jesus the entire way.

When Jesus gets home, the two men walk into the Lord's

home uninvited. Up to this point, they display their belief in Jesus as the Messiah. They even use the messianic term *Son of David*. They obviously are tenacious and willing to break the social norms. Perhaps something is missing, though.

In the four stories leading up to this passage found in Matthew 9:27–31, people willingly confess their belief in Jesus to perform miracles. In Matthew 8:2, the leper expresses his faith by saying, "Lord, if you are willing, you can make me clean." The centurion declares in Matthew 8:8, "But just say the word, and my servant will be healed." In Matthew 9:18, the official confesses publicly that if Jesus will go and lay his hand on his daughter, she will live. The woman with the issue of bleeding says to herself in Matthew 9:21, "If I only touch his cloak, I will be healed." However, the story of the two blind men is the only one in the New Testament where Jesus asks the question, *do you believe I can do this?* It's the only place where he requires the suppliants to proclaim their faith.

They respond without hesitation, "Why, yes, Master." Their declaration cements what they believe in their hearts. The verbalization makes their beliefs public, which is quite different than simply begging for mercy. It moves them from belief to conviction so that they can become what they truly believe.

That's when Jesus stretches out his hands and touches their eyes. His physical touch gives the two men more intimate contact with their healer. As Jesus does this, he makes the powerful proclamation, "Become what you believe" (Matt. 9:29, THE MESSAGE). At that moment, something happens that has never happened in their lives. Their optical nerves begin to transmit signals to their brains. Immediately, they begin to see perfectly.

Once their eyes were opened, Jesus gave them a stern warning, "Don't let a soul know how this happened" (Matt. 9:30,

THE MESSAGE). The term warned fiercely, as it appears in the Greek, represents a verb that occurs only here in Matthew.[1] Also, this is the only place we see in Matthew where the explicit order was not obeyed. Although no one knows why Jesus told them to keep the miracle quiet, two things stand out about these two blind men. First, they are the first in Matthew to address Jesus as Messiah, and he may have wanted to keep that fact from public knowledge until God's perfect time. Second, they were blind, yet recognized Jesus as the Messiah. Once their eyes were opened, they could physically identify him to the crowds and authorities.

It's Time to Ask Yourself What You Truly Believe

True beliefs eventually lead to convictions. Convictions lead us to action, which usually entails verbalizing our thoughts. When we open our mouths to speak, something happens in our minds that reaffirms and strengthens our beliefs. That is why couples during a wedding ceremony confess their commitment to each other before witnesses. That is why we must verbally take an oath before testifying in a court of law. And that is precisely why Paul states, "That if you confess with your mouth, 'Jesus is Lord,' and believe in your heart that God raised him from the dead, you will be saved. For it is with your heart that you believe and are justified, and it is with your mouth that you confess and are saved" (Rom. 10:9–10). As people of integrity, our confession makes public what is in our heart, and it ties us to what we believe.

Let me ask you a couple of questions about this important step in understanding New Testament faith. What *do* you believe? Is there something you hold to be overwhelmingly true that you would be willing to proclaim publicly? Would you, like African, Latin, and Asian believers, proclaim without hesitancy your belief that God heals, delivers, and divinely intervenes in our lives? Could you do that on the street before strangers or in front of an indifferent television host on a late night talk show? Could you confess your beliefs in front of your schoolmates, coworkers, or family members who don't believe as you do?

One reason miracles happen in other parts of the world is people have a conviction that Jesus will heal them. They not only believe it in theory, but their belief drives them to action. In essence their belief in the miraculous has become a conviction. In North America and Western Europe, we tend to live in a theoretical world of faith. I use the word *theoretical* because we normally do not let our belief in the supernatural heavily impact our practical everyday life. As Christians, we tend to believe Jesus came, died, and rose from the dead. We are not necessarily willing to go out on a limb in a university class and proclaim those tenets. We believe that Jesus healed the sick and performed mighty wonders. We even go so far as to believe that he can do so again whenever he desires. We tend not to open our mouths and say that God will heal or deliver or do the impossible. We hope he will, but when faced with the pressure of making a public stance, we become reluctant. To me, this suggests that our faith has not moved from theory to conviction for which we are willing to take a public stand. In other parts of the world this is not so much the case. This is what distinctly separates them from us. They, much like the little boy that jumps to his father in the pool, hardly doubt that God will intervene when they need him.

The concept of moving from belief to conviction was not foreign to Jesus. He understood just how important it was. Mark

9 illustrates this vital point. As Jesus came upon a crowd arguing with his disciples, a man brought his son before the Lord and explained his serious condition. An evil spirit possessed the boy and robbed him of speech. The spirit would throw the boy to the ground in convulsions, causing him to foam at the mouth and gnash his teeth. Then the boy would become rigid. After the disciples couldn't drive out the evil spirit, the father asked Jesus to help.

"'O unbelieving generation,' Jesus replied, 'how long shall I stay with you? How long shall I put up with you? Bring the boy to me'" (Mark 9:19). As soon as the spirit saw Jesus, it threw the boy into a violent convulsion. As the boy rolled around on the ground and foamed at the mouth, Jesus turned to the father and asked, "How long has he been like this?" This question, which is often overlooked, sheds light on another spiritual truth that has taken me years to discover. It is my experience that the longer someone has battled a sickness or ailment, the more embedded the sickness becomes. To a large degree, it becomes part of the person's identity and thus more difficult to break. Jesus' question has to do with finding out to what degree the boy's demon possession has become part of his identity.

"From childhood," the father answered. "It has often thrown him into fire or water to kill him. But if you can do anything, take pity on us and help us." "'If you can'?" said Jesus. "Everything is possible for him who believes" (Mark 9:21–23). Jesus obviously is taken back by the man's apparent internal struggle. You see, the father wasn't asking Jesus to heal his son because he was convinced, like the centurion in Luke 7 or the synagogue ruler Jairus in Mark 5:22. Instead, the father asked the Lord if there was anything he could do for the boy, much like when we take a car to the mechanic after the engine blows up.

We may not be sure if the mechanic can rebuild the engine, but we'll ask him to give it a shot. This is why Jesus repeated the man's words, "If you can?" Again, Jesus only does this once in his ministry. The man's answer indicates that he is not quite certain that Jesus is capable of healing his son.

The verse that follows powerfully demonstrates the struggle of a father trying to believe. "I do believe; help me overcome my unbelief!" (Mark 9:24). He is crying out for help, for someone to help him move from uncertainty to total belief. As Jesus sees the crowd growing, he casts the evil spirit out of the boy and lifts him to his feet.

How can someone believe and yet struggle with unbelief? The father's confession reminds me of thousands of conversations I've had over the years. Many people want to believe and may even believe that miracles are possible. But their beliefs have not transitioned into convictions. Just like the boy's father, many people live between two stages of faith, the theoretical and the practical. What about you? In which stage of faith do you live? Is your faith theoretical or has it become a conviction that guides your actions? If you see yourself in the boy's father, the following section will help you move from uncertainty to conviction.

What We Can Do to Change

A belief is something that is supported by experience and knowledge. When you ask yourself why you believe something, references and experience come to mind as support for your belief. I hesitate to use the word *evidence* in this case because it depicts something that can be gathered, quantified, and dissected in a lab. Faith is a spiritual trait, not a scientific one.

So as we gather greater support and references that help form what we believe, our beliefs become more powerful. For example, if you believe that Jesus rose from the dead, it's healthy to look at the many different references and occurrences where he appeared to people after his resurrection. The more you understand what historians wrote about the risen Christ and the eyewitness accounts of what took place, the stronger your belief becomes. Eventually, you visualize it. You see it. And your belief becomes so strong that it transitions into a conviction.

The same is true of miracles, revivals, signs, and wonders. With the support we gather, our beliefs become convictions that cause us to verbalize that God will do the same in our lives. As we discussed in chapter 3, many people in the New Testament heard the reports about Jesus before meeting him. Those references built their beliefs so that they were convinced prior to their encounter with Jesus. Without hesitancy, they verbalized their belief that Jesus would do the miracle before it occurred.

Perhaps you're asking, *how can I strengthen my beliefs?* The first thing you can do is spend time with those whose beliefs have become convictions about their faith. The people groups I've mentioned (Latin American, African, and Asian Christians) carry a conviction that God continues to do the miraculous today. Listen to their stories. See how they view the supernatural world. Try to gain their insights on faith and being a disciple. As the saying goes, birds of a feather flock together. When you spend time with people, their influence eventually rubs off on you. So let people with New Testament faith influence the way you see the world.

Second, read material from trusted and reliable sources that will help build your beliefs. Craig Keener's book *Miracles,* which I mentioned in the introduction of this book, is a scholarly work that documents how miracles are happening all around the world, even in Western Europe and North America.[2] Read testimonies of miracles published by major denominations, such as the Assemblies of God's *The Pentecostal Evangel* or other periodicals that document miracles.[3] When you hear reports that have no logical explanation aside from God's intervention, your faith will be strengthened.

Third, spend time in prayer and examine the miracle stories in the Bible. Ask the Lord to open your eyes to see miracles in your life. Many times, miracles happen all around us, but we are unaware or fail to recognize them. As you pray, God will open your eyes to see the supernatural things he is orchestrating. Then, as you read God's Word, remember each of the miracle stories had a significant impact on people's lives. Many people died for their faith in God because of the miracles they witnessed. So be careful not to dismiss a story such as the parting of the Red Sea, the feeding of the five thousand, or Jesus' resurrection simply because it doesn't seem possible. If those people who died for their faith endured horrific deaths, it's probably because they were convinced as eyewitnesses that those miracles took place. I am convinced that if you genuinely seek the Lord in these things, he will guide you. When you see his hand performing miracles, it will encourage and edify you. Then be faithful to spread the word.

Finally, be fair. Sometimes, aspirin cures a headache. Sometimes, God does. Sometimes, God empowers a doctor, a scientist in a lab, or a paramedic to make the right choice at the right moment and our lives are extended another thirty years. If there is a logical explanation, then don't over-spiritualize things. Give credit where credit is due.

As we bring this chapter to a close, remember that the people who experience miracles around the world like those in the New Testament have a conviction that God will heal, deliver, and intervene in their lives. Whenever prompted, they are more than willing to verbalize publicly their faith in God before the miracle takes place. Their faith is not simply theoretical, it's practical, and it affects every area of their lives. In Western Europe and North America, our faith has drifted from a practical way of living to a theoretical one. It has become disconnected from the way we conduct our lives and thus our faith has not become a conviction.

We can break this pattern by spending more time with those who carry deep convictions that miracles happen frequently. Many times, those individuals come from other parts of the world. We can pick up trustworthy resources that document miracles as well as spend time in prayer to ask God to open our eyes. If you truly seek the good deeds that the Lord is orchestrating, you will find them. Allow your beliefs to become convictions, and over time you will *become what you believe*.

I am convinced that prayer is our starting point whenever we need God's power. If you are looking for a miracle and you need God's intervention, the following prayer will help you verbalize to the Lord what we've learned in this chapter.

Father, I ask you to open my eyes to see miracles in my life. I know there are many competing ideas in my head, but I ask you to give me clarity of mind. Help my beliefs to become convictions so that I am willing to take action and move in your direction. Give me the strength to open my mouth and publically verbalize my faith in you even before I see any evidence that the miracle is on its way.

I pray you would open the floodgates of heaven and pour out your Spirit upon me. I want to see your healing. I desire to see your divine provision. I yearn to experience your deliverance. And when these miracles occur, help me to embrace them and not dismiss them. I commit to be vigilant and to give you all the glory. In Christ's name, I pray. Amen.

Questions for discussion or personal reflection

1. Describe the most impressive miracle you've experienced, read about, or heard of.

2. What areas of your faith have moved from a simple belief to a conviction?

3. Is this conviction something so moving that you would be willing to talk about it on a secular television program or in a university classroom?

4. In what ways would verbalizing your faith that God will do a miracle make you feel uncomfortable? In what ways would it empower you?

5. How does verbalizing your belief in the Lord to do miracles strengthen your faith?

Chapter Seven
A Spirit of Bravado

Recently, I received a letter from Alex, someone dear to my heart. A resident of Central America, Alex has had a profound impact on me. I felt I should paraphrase his letter for you. He said that when he was eleven years old, his home was filled with dysfunction and pain. He had no father. He had no role model. The family lived in extreme poverty in a marginalized community. They would go for days without food. At Christmas time, there were no gifts, no tree, no special meal, and no celebration. His mother was forced into prostitution just to put food on their table.

Life for Alex was meaningless and empty, so he turned to drugs to numb the pain. Time and time again, he combined pills in an attempt to take his own life, but nothing worked. Then one day he heard of an event called "There is hope in Jesus." It was an evangelistic campaign coming to his town. He said to himself, "If God can turn lives around, perhaps he can turn mine around." That's when boldness replaced his attitude of defeat.

When he walked onto the crusade lot, he heard me speak of how I came from a crazy family and how God can turn anyone around. "With Christ there is hope for anyone," I said. "No one is exempt." That phrase was medicine for his soul. When I gave the altar call, Alex walked forward and accepted Christ as his savior. Suddenly, the heaviness that weighed him down lifted, and his mind became clear. With an overwhelming desire to forgive his parents for their abuse and mistakes, he lifted his arms to heaven and said, "God, forgive me for my sin, as I also forgive those who have sinned against me."

That day, Christ completely revolutionized the life of an eleven-year-old boy who lived in a marginalized neighborhood filled with conflict and anguish. That was just the beginning, however. Alex went on to lead other members of his family to Christ. With a spirit of bravado, he boldly proclaimed the power of God to others in his neighborhood as well. He now travels the country speaking and holding meetings like the one in which he found Christ. He sees miracles. He experiences the same breakthroughs the disciples witnessed. Today, he is the worship director in his church and has completely broken the cycle that held his mother and family in chains.

Many times we underestimate the significance of a strong spirit that is willing to do whatever it takes to overcome what we face. When the Lord sees tenacity, his heart is moved with compassion to intervene. The seventh characteristic found in those who experience the miraculous is a *spirit of bravado*. Christians in Asia, Africa, and Latin America, like those in the New Testament, are more than willing to break social norms and certain laws to receive from the Lord what they believe is their solution. They strive, fight, and literally do what it takes to get close to the source of their miracle. They display an extraordinary amount of *guts*. In essence, they are willing to take a huge risk, while at the same time push their pride to one side.

Please don't misunderstand what I am suggesting. There is a significant difference between being persistent and being rude. These people who experience miracles find a way to be bold without being out of control. They consistently bang on heaven's door and somehow avoid infuriating the Lord. They instinctively know the limit and dance along that fine line without crossing it.

A perfect example of this tenacity is found in Jesus' parable in Luke 18:1–8. In a certain town there was a judge who didn't fear God or people. Every day a widow came to him pleading her case and begging him to grant her justice against her adversary. For a time, he refused to help her. Suddenly, he had a change of heart, not because of compassion but because he could tell that her persistence would drive him crazy. He said to himself, "Even though I don't fear God or care about men, yet because this widow keeps bothering me, I will see that she gets justice, so that she won't eventually wear me out with her coming!" (Luke 18:5). I like the way Joel Green portrays the battle that takes place between the widow and the unjust judge. Green writes, "She is acting so out of station that, he muses, she may even be capable of assaulting him with more than words! The language Luke uses is startling, perhaps even humorous, borrowed as it is from the boxing ring, for it invokes images of the almighty, fearless, macho judge cornered and slugged by the least powerful in society."[1] It seems that the widow is having not only an emotional toll on the judge but a physical one as well.

Then Jesus urges his listeners, "Listen to what the unjust judge says. And will not God bring about justice for his chosen ones, who cry out to him day and night? Will he keep putting them off? I tell you, he will see that they get justice, and quickly. However, when the Son of Man comes, will he find faith on the earth?" (Luke 18:6–8).

Here we see Jesus emphasizing God's faithfulness in response to those who consistently call on his name. Notice that the judge in the story does not indicate that the woman is acting inappropriately. All she wants is justice. Obviously, she can't afford to pay a bribe. She can't afford counsel. She has no man to go before the judge on her behalf. So whatever legal work must be done to move her case before the judge she has to do herself. She is willing to do so persistently, consistently, and relentlessly until he finally grants her request.

This is the attitude that God rewards. The Bible says that God rewards those who seek him. Jesus says in Luke 11:9, "So I say to you: Ask and it will be given to you; seek and you will find; knock and the door will be opened to you." Hebrews 11:6 says, "And without faith it is impossible to please God, because anyone who comes to him must believe that he exists and that he rewards those who earnestly seek him." Do you have the qualities of the widow? Or does your pride and lack of patience keep you from knocking on heaven's door for weeks, months, or even years on end?

Humble Tenacity

Wherever there are healings, miracles, signs, and wonders, there are people who are bold and daring. They humbly and confidently ask God to intervene in their lives. This is true in Asia, Africa, and Latin America. I am one missionary among 4,500 in just one denomination who work around the world. My wife and I have dedicated most of our ministry years to Latin America. Our colleagues who work in Africa and Asia see the same phenomena. Their stories are similar to those in our region. They reflect many of the same miracles that took place in the New Testament.

Of all the countries in the Western Hemisphere in which I've had the honor and privilege of preaching, the church in Cuba is perhaps the closest to the New Testament church that we see in the Book of Acts. Believers in Cuba do not have the resources that believers have in other areas. Yet, they are not politically focused. They recognize that God is their one and only source for everything in life. They have great faith and have personally taught me much about what you are reading in this book. In Cuba, the average salary isn't astronomical. Yet, in spite of the adversity and challenge they face, the Christians of Cuba build church buildings that can hold hundreds of people and can withstand the forces of some of the most powerful hurricanes to date. Their churches are self-supporting, self-propagating, and self-governing. The first thing you will notice about believers in the island nation is their extreme commitment to biblical Christianity. Cuban Christians display great faith and joy. They definitely display a strong spirit of bravado and boldness that impel them to pursue God's miracles, provision, and deliverance even to the edges of what is socially acceptable.

Recently, I spoke at a youth congress in Havana, Cuba. The service started at 8:00 p.m. with great music and beautiful soloists. Inside the building, it was still ninety degrees with high humidity. Some came prepared with hand fans that provided a gentle breeze to relieve the nearly unbearable heat. Eventually, I began preaching the sermon at 9:45 p.m. I spoke for thirty minutes and gave an altar call. Hundreds flocked to the altar. By the time we finished praying with those who made a first-time commitment to Christ and for those who needed a miracle, it was 11:15 p.m. Needless to say, I was tired.

As I walked across the dirt road and got into the minivan that would take me to my lodging for the night, a woman approached the driver's window and said, "I must speak to Jason." The driver replied, "We're leaving now. Jason will be glad to meet with you before the service tomorrow." She said, "It's urgent. Please, I must see him tonight. Have him get out of the vehicle and pray for my situation." There was no doubt about her determination. So I stepped out of the minivan and asked how I might be of assistance. "Please pray for my grandson," she said. "He's been here each night. He can't read. He has a learning disability, and his teachers and doctors can't help him. We need a miracle!"

The grandmother wasn't rude or disrespectful, but she pushed social norms to their limits. When someone says, "We're leaving. Come back tomorrow," most people turn away. Those with a spirit of bravado are willing to push beyond the limits because they are convinced that God will answer their petition.

If you look at the history of the church in Cuba in the last one hundred years, you will see the thousands upon thousands of documented miracles, explosive church growth, and unprecedented dedication to the proclamation of the Gospel. All these things are the result of an unwavering New Testament faith. In many ways they're a modern day example of what we see in the story found in Luke 5:12–14.

In the story, a man covered with leprosy comes before Jesus and falls to his knees, begging Jesus to heal him. With his face to the ground he says, "Lord, if you are willing, you can make me clean" (Luke 5:12). This statement is rather ambiguous. It is unclear if he is asking Jesus to cure him of his disease or to declare him clean. Being cured of leprosy in biblical times was a two-step process. Once someone received a cure for the disease, he had to go to the priest and offer sacrifices. Once the sacrificial requirements were met, the priest could declare the person clean, so he could re-enter society. Without final clearance a leper by law had to stay in isolation. Further, it was against the law for a leper to wander the streets and mix with the general public, because it would expose many people to the deadly disease.

The leper's actions in this instance were bold, tenacious, and even dangerous. What's even more intriguing is Jesus' response. The man doesn't ask Jesus to touch him, but that is in fact what Jesus does. He reaches out, touches the man, and says, "I am willing. Be clean!" (v. 13). Immediately the leprosy left him. Luke's retelling illustrates that Jesus not only cures the man of his disease, but by touching him shows him acceptance back into society.[2]

Then the Lord takes it one step further. He orders the man not to tell a soul until he shows himself to the priest. Jesus tells him to offer the sacrifices that Moses commanded for his cleansing as a testimony to them. Then, the priest would declare the man cured in order for him to return to society. Thus, Jesus fulfills the law after breaking the norm of touching a man covered with leprosy.

There's no doubt the leper had guts. He was willing to push the rules of society to their limits, and God rewarded his faith. Much like our friends in other parts of the world, he was willing to take a risk to see the hand of God move in his life. What about Western Europe and North America? Do we see this type of faith and tenacity? Or does individual pride or fear impede our ability to go beyond the social norm. Are we willing, as the two blind men were, to follow Jesus a great distance and then walk into his home uninvited? Now don't get me wrong. I am not suggesting that you stalk people or burst into their homes hoping they will pray for you. There is a difference between being tenacious and being creepy. But there is a way for you to stand up and say what Jacob said to the Lord: "I will not let you go until you bless me!" That same spirit of bravado is something found in many of those who received miracles in the New Testament as well as those around the world today. I believe you too can receive a miracle if you pursue God with the same tenacity as they do.

What To Do in the Face of *No*

The second question I am asked more then any other by North Americans and Western Europeans is *what do I do if my prayers are not answered?* I've worked with Hispanics full-time since 1991. I cannot remember one of them ever asking me what we do if God doesn't answer our prayers. This puts me in a unique position. Because I can understand both worlds, I can experience the joy of revival in Latin America as well as see the potential for revival in spite of the spiritual dryness that many believers experience in the United States. My desire at this important crossroad is to help you move forward from a place where you may feel stuck.

First and foremost, please remember that you are in a process. Revival doesn't come in a day. Great faith doesn't manifest itself out of nowhere. Great spiritual movements come out of tribulation, frustration, and many times out of sorrow and pain. The places we have discussed in this book where revival is occurring are either in the midst of great conflict, or they are exiting from one. So allow God to guide you through the process, even when it is difficult.

Second, there are many times in the New Testament when the Lord is either silent or doesn't seem to pay attention. While it is easy for us to think that God doesn't care, he uses those times to test our faith. He wants to see how dedicated we are. So when it seems as though God is not answering your prayers, be persistent. Don't simply pray once and forget about it. Ask the Lord regularly for what you need. That is why Paul urges us

1 Thessalonians 5:17 to never stop praying.

Third, enroll others in your prayer task force. Don't take on your trials and tribulations alone. Ask others to pray with you and to believe God for miracles to occur in your life. The Bible says, "I also tell you this: If two of you agree here on earth concerning anything you ask, my Father in heaven will do it for you. For where two or three gather together as my followers, I am there among them." (Matt. 18:19–20, NLT-SE).

Fourth, keep track of the prayers that God is answering in a prayer journal. When you see over time how God answers your prayers, it will strengthen your faith in powerful ways. You will also get a sense of God's timing. This will enable you to see how long it takes before you receive an answer.

Finally, decide to glorify the Lord regardless of where he leads you in life. Paul had what he termed a thorn in the flesh given to him by a messenger of Satan. No one really knows what it was, but Paul asked the Lord to remove it from him on several occasions. For some reason, God did not. And when Paul asked why, the Lord replied, "My grace is sufficient for you." Paul learned that through it all, he had to glorify God with his life, no matter what the outcome. God's grace was all that Paul really needed.

Moses understood this as well. After being born in poverty, Moses grew up in the palace of Egypt, the superpower of its time. Then at age forty, he lost everything and fled for his life. By the time he was eighty, God finally called him to return to Egypt. Imagine taking forty years to prepare to experience the miraculous. God used Moses to bring Egypt to its knees, and to free his fellow Israelites from Egyptian slavery. Because of a lack of faith in God's power, the Israelites wandered in the desert for another forty years. They experienced one process and one delay after another, followed by one painful lesson and setback after another. Still, God never left them until one day when he finally had enough. God said to Moses, "That's it. I'm done. I will not go with you any further."

That's when Moses, who had asked God to guide the Israelites into the Promised Land, came to the most important reality of his life. He said to the Lord, "If your Presence does not go with us, do not send us up from here" (Exod. 33:15). In other words, God, you are much more important than the Promised Land, the miracles, and anything we could hope to glean in that land. Moses' attitude, I believe, puts things in proper perspective for us. In the face of losing the most important thing in his life, he chose to ask God for the one thing he couldn't deny. So if you believe that your prayers are not being answered, ask God for the one thing he will never deny you—his love and presence. After all, that is his most precious gift.

Our prayers should reflect an attitude that says, *you may not grant me what I want, but please don't leave me. I don't want to move forward without your presence. You, my Lord, are worth so much more to me than the gifts I receive from you*. That is a prayer to which God will never say no. With this type of heart and attitude, it wasn't a surprise to see the Lord's response to Moses' plea. "And the LORD said to Moses, 'I will do the very thing you have asked, because I am pleased with you and I know you by name'" (Exod. 33:17).

Looking at Moses' attitude is perhaps the best way we can bring this chapter to a close. I know that it can be frustrating to feel that God is not answering your prayers. In spite of the frustrations, I want to encourage you. I pray that God would allow you to experience the joy of seeing him work in your life in a convincing way. I pray that in the midst of your storms that you will clearly see the hand of God. May he grant you the miracles, healing, and breakthrough you need today and in the days to come. May your faith rise so that you will *become what you believe*. I trust that the following prayer will be a catalyst for such a breakthrough.

> *Father, I ask you to move in my life in a clear and convincing way. Help me to do what it takes and to have the faith necessary to keep knocking on heaven's door. I recognize you as the source of all good things in my life. I do not want to be pushy, but I do want to be persistent. I don't want to be rude, but I do want to be determined.*
>
> *Help me to know when I should continue to pray or when it's time to change the way that I pray. I don't want to pray against your will, but I do want to be someone of great faith. Help me to pray in such away that your hand begins to move in my life. I ask you to help me experience a significant breakthrough in the coming days and weeks. I ask these things in your precious and holy name. Amen.*

Questions for discussion or personal reflection

1. In what ways do you find balance between being pushy (or even rude) and persistent and tenacious when it comes to your prayer life?

2. Describe someone you know who displays a spirit of bravado when it comes to matters of faith. In what ways does that person display tenacity and persistence? In what ways do they display faith?

3. Have you ever felt that your prayers haven't been answered?

4. Have you ever had a strong sense of desperation that led you to go beyond social norms in order to get what you felt you needed? Describe the scenario.

Chapter Eight
PERSISTENT EVEN WHEN IGNORED

As I sat across the table from one of the national church leaders in an African nation I mentioned that another pastor from his country had asked if I could acquire large-print Bibles for him. The pastor replied, "You have no idea how scarce they are!" I said, "Do you mean to tell me there are no large-print Bibles in this country?" He said, "Not only that, but we hardly have any regular Bibles." Apparently, importing Bibles was more difficult than I was aware.

After dinner, I headed to another service and spoke in a house church where approximately one hundred people gathered in a makeshift living room. The circulating fans blew the hot humid air tinged with human body odor from one end of the room to the other. I shared the story of the paralyzed man in John 5. Afterward, I asked if anyone needed healing, and I was surprised to see around eighty people raise their hands. We prayed as a group, because there was no room for an altar call. I gave the pastor the microphone, and he asked the crowd, "How many of you would like to share the miracle that God has done in your body tonight?"

I was shocked to see people literally fighting over the microphone to have an opportunity to share what the Lord had done. One lady said, "I had a lump in my breast. I couldn't even touch it without experiencing pain and discomfort. The lump is completely gone!" Then without shame or embarrassment, she grabbed her breast and squeezed it in front of everyone and said, "See? Look what the Lord did!" I just closed my eyes while others covered their mouths and laughed. An elderly woman bent over and touched her toes. "I couldn't do this for years," she said. The crowd erupted into applause.

Finally, a woman in her seventies walked forward and said, "Pastor, you know that I have not been able to see well enough to read my Bible in a decade. I've asked God to heal me for years. After praying tonight something happened. All of a sudden, I could see clearly. Please hand me your Bible." The small-print Bible was a challenge even for me to read, and I have 20/20 vision. The woman opened the Bible to one of the Gospels and began reading a story without missing a single word. The pastor said, "I can't read this Bible without my reading glasses." The woman's healing clearly illustrates the patience that millions of people in other parts of the world have. They wait on God for miracles and do not misconstrue his silence. Their persistence helps them not lose hope in what we would consider to be a hopeless cause. In short, they hang in there until they believe God has rendered his *final* decision.

Many times, we become discouraged over God's silence, thinking that it's an indication that he is ignoring us, is bothered by our petitions, or doesn't care. God's uncommunicativeness isn't a form of torture or rudeness. He isn't being mean. He is simply testing our faith. Much as when a muscle faces resistance and becomes stronger, our faith gains strength when it is tested. So our persistence in the midst of God's silence allows us to take one step closer to becoming what we believe.

The eighth characteristic found in those who experience the miraculous is the quality of being *persistent even when the Lord seems to ignore them*. Much like those in the New Testament who wouldn't mistake Christ's silence for rejection, Christians in Asia, Africa, and Latin America display a significant amount of persistence. In North America and Western Europe, the idea of continuously seeking God for something even though he has maintained silence for an extended period of time is foreign to us. Many would assume that if God hasn't responded by now, then he probably won't. In contrast, people in the New Testament have a completely different mindset. They don't take the Lord's silence as rejection. Instead, they see it for what it is, a test of their faith.

There is a beautiful story that illustrates this point in Matthew 15. After Jesus leaves the region known as Gennesaret, he withdraws to the region of Tyre and Sidon. There a Phoenician woman comes near, crying out, "Lord, Son of David, have mercy on me! My daughter is suffering terribly from demon-possession" (Matt. 15:22). Matthew makes a point to state that the woman was from that area and was a Gentile and not a Jew. For centuries, the Jews and Canaanites were enemies. The Lord offers no response to her plea. After a short time, her persistence is more than the disciples can handle. They know the only way the woman will leave is if Jesus says something to her. So they intervene.

"Send her away, for she keeps crying out after us," they say (v. 23). Again, Jesus refuses to say anything to her. Instead, Jesus turns and addresses the disciples. "I was sent only to the lost sheep of Israel" (v. 24). His words draw a line in the sand that marks the division between Jew and Gentile that existed for thousands of years. Although he is not speaking to her, she hears him clearly, comes closer, and kneels before him.

"Lord, help me!" she begs. Without pausing Jesus replies, "It is not right to take the children's bread and toss it to their dogs" (v. 26). What a response! Locking horns with Jesus is not for the faint of heart. Let me be clear about something. I can assure you that dogs are dogs in any culture except in North

America and Western Europe, where society puts up billboards that read, "Pets are people, too." Calling someone a dog outside of our pet-loving culture is an insult—even more so two thousand years ago. It would seem that Jesus is adding insult to injury.

Or was he setting up the Phoenician woman? Perhaps he was testing her faith while teaching the disciples a valuable lesson about faith and the extent of his plan of salvation.

At that moment, the woman could have turned and sorrowfully walked away. Her story would have ended there, and her daughter's fate would have been sealed. Instead, her response would mark the difference in the lives of hundreds of millions of people around the world. "Yes, Lord," she said, "but even the dogs eat the crumbs that fall from their masters' table" (v. 27). I like the way R. T. France sums up what she has done: "She turns Jesus' own parable against him. If Gentiles are to be 'dogs,' then at least let the dogs have their due. The dogs do have a right to be fed, even if all they get is the leftovers."[1] To such a faith-filled response Jesus answered, "Woman, you have great faith! Your request is granted" (v. 28). Immediately, her daughter was healed. Jesus' answer depicts an attitude of joy. It was as if he were saying, "You've passed the test! As a matter of fact, you did better than my disciples and all the people of Israel."

Several important observations regarding this story are worth highlighting. First, in the synoptic Gospels, only twice does Jesus send a word of healing to someone who is sick. This woman's daughter is one. The centurion's servant is the other. Both are Gentiles.

Second, Jesus gives each suppliant the highest compliment regarding faith. He said to the woman, "You have great faith," and to the centurion, "I have not found such great faith even in Israel." In contrast, in the chapters leading up to this story, Jesus refers to the disciples as having *little faith,* as being *dull,* and *not understanding* the simplest of parables. Indeed, Matthew shows us a powerful contrast between the disciples (religious people) and the foreigners.

Third, neither the woman nor centurion received the miracle. Rather, they are interceding on behalf of someone they love, and the Lord grants their request. This comes as good news to us. People who have great faith can intercede on our behalf when we are weak. Or we can intercede for others who are unable to approach the Lord. The Lord's healing powers are not limited by physical distance or by the fact that the one in need isn't capable of asking.

Fourth, the mother in Matthew 15 not only passed the test, but she became the first Gentile in the book of Matthew to experience salvation. With her, God's plan became clear. Salvation is not based on race or nationality. It's based on faith in Christ.

A Different Spiritual Mindset

As a missionary evangelist working overseas for nearly twenty-five years, I have discovered that people who live where God is doing the miraculous have a different spiritual DNA than those who live in Western Europe and North America. They see things differently, and they hear things differently. For example, when God seems to be silent, we Westerners interpret that as a negative answer. Our Christian friends in Africa, Asia, and Latin America read God's silence differently than we do. And because of that, they respond to him differently.

In a sense, it's like floating on the surface of the water.

When we lie back in the water and relax, we can float all day long. Similarly, people with New Testament faith don't need to fight or expend significant amounts of energy to believe God's promises or trust him. When faced with silence or seeming setbacks, their spiritual mindset helps them float back to the surface. It directs them to the source of their miracle. Instead of sinking in despair, they find hope and gravitate to the Lord.

A close friend from Costa Rica had this type of mindset. Back in the 1970s, he and his wife tried for five years to have a child. The doctors told them there wasn't anything they could do. So the couple started to attend a church plant campaign called La Gran Campaña de Sanidad Divina (The Great Campaign of Divine Healing) in Moravia, Costa Rica. Each night for another five years, they walked forward and prayed with everyone else, believing God for a miracle. You would think that after ten years, they would have given up. Instead, each time they heard the testimonies of others, it only strengthened their faith and inspired them. They never mistook God's silence for rejection. Instead of falling into despair or discouragement, they kept saying, "One day, our miracle will come! One day, we'll have a baby!" Finally, the Lord responded. My friend's wife became pregnant. Then two years later, she had a second child.

I also could tell you about how the faith of a child resembles persistence in the face of being ignored. When my family and I left Costa Rica in 2005, we not only left a home and friends, we also left two dogs that our daughters loved. Each of our daughters felt a significant loss, especially our youngest daughter, Jazmin. For years, she wanted another dog to replace the German Shepherd she had adored. She begged, pleaded, and promised she would take care of the dog. To say that Cindee and I were opposed is an understatement. We were adamantly against the idea. I kept saying, "We travel. We don't have a yard. Plus, we can't be tied down!" All I could envision was a home in disarray, a backyard full of the stench of feces, chewed shoes, half-eaten furniture, and dog hair everywhere. Not only did Jazmin want a dog, she wanted a big one. For several years, I sounded like a broken record, *no, no, no*.

About six years ago, I was speaking on this topic, and Jazmin came up to me after the service and said, "Dad, do you really believe that God opens doors for those who have faith?"

I said, "Of course I do."

She said, "Well, I want to ask you to pray for an open door for me."

"Sure, sweetheart," I said. "How can I pray for you?"

She said, "Please pray about getting the right dog for our family."

"No way!" I responded. "I don't have to pray about that!"

She asked, "You don't care if God has a special dog for our family?"

In my head, I really didn't care. However, since I had just preached on faith, I thought that I should display a good attitude and show some support. So I reluctantly agreed to pray about the idea. As a parting shot I said, "Don't think that I don't see what you're trying to do. I really don't think that God cares about whether we get a dog or not."

After praying several times, Cindee and I found ourselves researching dog shelter websites. Within two weeks, we went to the shelter and got the dog Jazmin prayed for. How did this happen? I've asked myself that many times. Simply put, her faith was resolute. The dog, Maggie, has been a wonderful pet for her, especially during some of the challenging times of her high school years.

Then again, I could tell you about a special person I met because of the time I spoke on the Crystal Cathedral's "Hour of Power" back in 2009 and 2010. This person did not attend the Crystal Cathedral, but was a television viewer. The viewer wrote me three years after my six episodes aired. Recently, I received a message on my Facebook page from a Pakistani woman. She asked for my e-mail address, saying that it was urgent. After I gave her my e-mail address, she sent me a crusade report with photographs of her open-air campaign. She travels around her country preaching in marginalized areas, presenting the Gospel to her Muslim nation. Her life is in danger, yet she continues to believe God for open doors and miracles.

As I began to look at the different pictures she sent, I was captivated by the humility of the Pakistani people. Hundreds upon hundreds of people met in an enclosed area surrounded by roofless block walls with nothing more than one or two floodlights illuminating the entire area. Tears streamed down their faces as they asked Christ to be their savior. It is obvious that such a bold step of faith could easily put their lives and family in jeopardy.

As I was about halfway through the attached photographs, I noticed that she had put up a projection screen, and everyone in the audience was fixated on the video she was showing. As I glanced at the image on the projection screen, at first I couldn't believe my eyes. It was me. She was showing the messages that I preached on "Hour of Power" three years earlier. After the video message ended, she stood up and gave an altar call for salvation, and scores of Pakistanis gave their hearts to Christ. She continues to hold evangelistic outreaches throughout the country. To date, over 8,351 Pakistanis have given their lives to

Christ through her outreaches and video sermons.

Along with crusade reports, the Pakistani woman also sent me photographs of burned down villages and homes where fellow Christians have suffered greatly at the hands of those who do not share their faith. In that country, Christians have been martyred for the cause of Christ. For years, believers have cried out to the Lord for a breakthrough. Where many people in North America and Western Europe would simply say that God is silent or has abandoned them, my Pakistani friend consistently sees God's hand of protection and backing. She has never given up hope and continues to wait on the Lord for every one of his provisions.

Yet in spite of the storms she faces, she has shared with me many testimonies of people in her meetings who were set free from demon possession, healed from physical illness, and delivered from religious persecution. They are living a New Testament moment. The miracles are countless, and the testimonies reflect what Jesus did two thousand years ago.

Once again, I am reminded of the woman in Luke 18 who we talked about in chapter 7, who wore down the unjust judge. With great persistence, she wouldn't take no for an answer. How much more is God just in comparison to a human unjust judge who doesn't care about people or fear the Lord? How much better will God treat those he loves? His silence doesn't last forever.

King David pleaded with the Lord not to keep silent. "O LORD, you have seen this; be not silent. Do not be far from me, O Lord" (Ps. 35:22). "O God, do not keep silent; be not quiet, O God, be not still" (Ps. 83:1). "To you I call, O LORD my Rock; do not turn a deaf ear to me. For if you remain silent, I will be like those who have gone down to the pit" (Ps. 28:1). Yet

David's spiritual mindset made him gravitate back to the Lord regardless of the silence or hardship. He said, "That my heart may sing to you and not be silent. O LORD my God, I will give you thanks forever" (Ps. 30:12).

Through it all, gravitate to the Lord. There will be times when you think that God has abandoned you. There will be moments when you think he is not there. You may feel your enemies are closing in. The point in this section is crucial. As long as you draw close to the Lord, he will draw close to you (James 4:8). He will never abandon you, nor will he ever forsake you. He makes these wonderful promises to you in his Word. "And surely I am with you always, to the very end of the age" (Matt. 28:20). "I will not leave you as orphans; I will come to you" (John 14:18). "So I say to you: Ask and it will be given to you; seek and you will find; knock and the door will be opened to you. For everyone who asks receives; he who seeks finds; and to him who knocks, the door will be opened" (Luke 11:9–10).

No-nonsense Commitment

When we look at the lives of those mentioned in this chapter in addition to those whose stories are threaded throughout the pages of this book, we see some interesting correlations. The two blind men in Matthew 9, who followed Jesus a great distance and went into his house uninvited, somehow dealt with his silence during their journey. Blind Bartimaeus called out to the Lord as he sat on the side of the road while those around him rebuked him and told him to keep quiet. Somehow, he dealt with the initial rejection. When the Lord refused to answer the woman who begged him to set her daughter free from demon possession, she somehow dealt with the insult of being put in the same category as a dog. All of these people, including my friends in Cuba and Pakistan, have something in common. The pain of staying the same was greater than the risk of humiliation. The reward of the miracle was worth taking the risk. Knocking on heaven's door cost them their pride. Asking the Lord for a miracle in the face of seeming rejection, silence, and even insult required them to dig deep to see just how badly they wanted their miracle. There was something even more costly, though. Doing nothing would have been a much greater price for every one of them. In each of their cases, they had a no-nonsense commitment to receive their miracle.

Think of the two blind men. Staying blind would have cost them much more than giving up their pride. They would have lived out the rest of their lives in darkness, never knowing the joy of having sight. The same is true for the woman whose daughter was demon possessed. Think of the pain, suffering, and torment her family would have endured if the mother gave up because it was beneath her to beg and plead for her daughter's life. Her daughter would never have known the joy of having a family and growing old with grandchildren. In the case of the woman in Cuba, having the ability to read God's Word was worth the price of pushing aside her pride and waiting on the Lord ten years for a miracle.

There are certain things worth fighting for, and there are certain needs worth sacrificing your pride for. Many times, God's test of faith requires that we sacrifice our pride. If we truly have a no-nonsense commitment, we will ultimately ask ourselves one of the most important questions as followers of Christ, Are we willing to lay aside our arrogance and humble ourselves?

This question leads us directly into the next chapter of this book. The Lord exalts the humble. He is opposed to those who are prideful and arrogant, but he loves those who aren't self-centered and who don't think too highly of themselves. Those who stood their ground with the Lord in the New Testament in the face of his silence and at times initial rejection were known by their *humble persistence*.

Friend, I encourage you to be persistent and humble. Knock on the door, but don't bang on it. Ask the Lord with consistency, but don't demand. Gravitate toward him but not with the motive of using him to get what you want. We should follow the Lord because he is worthy. We shouldn't try to make deals with God. Instead, we follow him regardless of what comes our way. Stephen, who died a martyr's death, understood that. The Apostle Paul did as well. Countless others managed to find the right balance of humble persistence. I pray that you do, too!

May the following prayer serve as a guide as you seek to find the humble persistence that you need to see the hand of God move. May the Lord move mountains in your life. May he open your eyes to see the next steps that lie before you and the direction you must take. May the Lord help you *become what you believe*. Turn the page and we'll ask the Lord together.

Lord, I ask that you open my eyes to see your mighty hand move. Help me to have the faith that moves mountains. I want to become someone wholeheartedly committed to you. Help me not to misunderstand your silence. I long to find the right balance between humility and persistence. I know you love me. I know you care. Help me to see your heart when I am in despair.

May you rebuke the hand of the enemy. When he fills my mind with lies and thoughts of discouragement, help me to remember the promises in your Word. Through the difficult times and victories, help me to remember that you will never leave me nor forsake me. You are always faithful. I ask for your miracle-working power to touch my life in an unmistakable way. In Christ's name, I pray. Amen.

Questions for discussion or personal reflection

1. In what ways have you felt that God has not listened to your prayers?

2. Did you ever sense that your challenges were not a priority for him? If so, in what way?

3. Describe a time when you felt that God was silent or when you were unable to discern his direction. How did you finally manage to discover his will?

4. In your own words, what is a humble person? What is a persistent person? How can you become both without ceasing to be the person God created you to be?

Chapter Nine
THE ONE THING GOD ALWAYS OPPOSES

I walked down the stairs after speaking on "Hour of Power" and headed into the series of ready rooms underneath the immense glass structure of the Crystal Cathedral. I immediately recognized an internationally acclaimed youth evangelist from Argentina, who was slipping on his jacket to speak in the Spanish service that immediately followed. His name is Dante Gebel, and he is arguably the most popular youth evangelist in the history of Latin America. In 2009, he agreed to move from his home in Florida to pastor the Hispanic church at the Crystal Cathedral although he, like me, is Pentecostal. The Crystal Cathedral was a church affiliated with the Reformed Church of America, with practices and doctrines distinctly different from our own. Still, Dante felt that God was calling him to take the 150-member congregation and reach as many people as possible. That is quite a step for someone who normally speaks to ninety thousand people in a stadium.

He saw me and said, "Jason, I was deeply moved by your message and the testimonies you shared on 'Hour of Power'." I was shocked that Dante remembered my name let alone my message. He said, "I would love to have you come and preach to the Spanish congregation." Now there's a big difference between those who say, "Hey, we need to get together some time," and those who actually make it happen. Some people extend invitations they have no intention of fulfilling and promises they have no intention of keeping. Dante is not one of those people.

Within several weeks, he called and asked me to speak at his leadership summit. From that time forward, we have become close friends. After four years, I've spoken for him many times, and even though the Crystal Cathedral (English congregation) is now closed, Dante continues to pastor the Hispanic congregation under the new name Favorday Church. Its members now number close to four thousand. They have broken every church growth model. They've moved four times in a year and a half, and each time they do they continue to grow. They don't have a strategy or try to impress people with technological wonders. They are simply being the church in their community.

One thing that strikes me about Dante is his sincere humility. Every time I meet with him, he expresses genuine gratitude that I would take time out of my schedule to spend with him. Claudio Freidzon, who pastors in Buenos Aires, Argentina, has the same attitude. Dante grew up in that church, and when I spoke at Claudio's church, he expressed his heartfelt gratitude that I would fly seven thousand miles to be with his thirty-thousand member church. Both of these men are catalysts for revival in Latin America, but you would never know it by their humble demeanor. Their feet are firmly planted on the ground, and they know that God is their one and only source. They are very much aware that their talent has little to do with what the Lord has done through them. One thing goes through my mind when I spend time with them. It's the same feeling I have when I am in Cuba with people who have a fraction of what you and I have but do considerably more in the Kingdom of God. That thought is, "Lord, I am not worthy."

The Gold Nugget Versus Bad Breath

Humility is one of those New Testament characteristics that

I see in those who receive miracles. I have received hundreds of e-mails from pastors in Uganda, the Congo, Burkina Faso, Kenya, and other African nations who have experienced inexplicably miraculous phenomena. Many of them have much larger ministries than I do. In some cases, they pastor tens of thousands of people, but they do not reflect any arrogance. This is important, because if these leaders are humble, their followers will have a healthy role model and will embrace humility as well. This is why this chapter deals with the need to have a *genuinely humble heart,* which is the ninth characteristic found in those who experience the miraculous. Humility is not something they conjure up. It's a part of who they are and the way they see themselves. God sees humility as a gold nugget that's found in the heart.

In contrast, we in Western Europe and North America have a reputation for being arrogant. Granted, Western civilization influences the rest of the world, enjoys a great economy, builds huge skyscrapers, assembles powerful armed forces, creates technological advancements, and has birthed mega churches. Despite all that, our arrogance doesn't gain us any favor with God. Why? Because he always opposes the proud (Prov. 3:34, James 4:6). The rest of the world sees the way we view ourselves, and it is obvious to them that we have an inflated view of our accomplishments. They may not say anything to our face. As a matter of fact, they wouldn't even mention it if we pressed them. But the average Latin American, Asian, and African thinks that the people of Western Europe and North America believe they are God's gift to humanity. Like it or not, that is the image we project to the rest of the world. Unfortunately, our self-important attitude spills over into Christian culture.

Christians in the United States must be careful not to think that our form of Christianity is better than what is lived out overseas. Pastors need to be careful not to think that people attend their church because of their dynamic sermons or their great leadership. Worship leaders need to view themselves accurately and with humility and guard against becoming performers. Their talents are not what build the church. If they were, it wouldn't be a church worth attending. We must remember that God builds the church (Ps. 127:1).

Don't get me wrong. I know that God has gifted many pastors to be orators and great communicators. After all, the Lord called them and it follows that he would equip them with the necessary gifts to fulfill that call. I love people in ministry and greatly admire their commitment.

As a matter of fact, I am a huge advocate for all the ministries of the local church, its members, and all who call themselves believers. Why? Because I understand the challenges they face. Ministry today in North America and Western Europe is much harder than it was thirty years ago.

It is fair to say, though, that secular culture has infiltrated the church. And many people serving in the body of Christ believe that the success they've experienced is due to something special they possess. Sadly, they've begun to believe their own press, and what keeps them believing that lie is pride.

Let me emphasize an underlying theme in this book that you may not have noticed. When there are no miracles, when people's lives are not transformed, when the power of God is not manifested, the church looks for other things to attract people. It looks for substitutes for the power of God. It tries to come up with intriguing gimmicks to fill the pews. Churches look to invest in state-of-the-art sound and lighting. They create programs to tickle the ears and spend exorbitant amounts of money to fill the void the power of God once occupied. The Church does whatever it can to try to replace the authenticity of the power of the Gospel. There are some churches that go so far as to involve themselves in the political process, because deep down inside they are desperate to grab onto any source of power they can, even if it's one that God warns us to avoid.

Unfortunately, when we substitute entertainment for God's power, we fail to deal with the underlying problem that people have in society—a spiritual lostness, sinful destructive patterns, diabolic oppression, extreme poverty, and physical sickness. And what is it that keeps us from tapping into God's power, the true remedy for these ailments? Pride! Like my dear colleague Raul Vargas says, "Pride is like bad breath. Everyone around knows you have it, except you."

Do I think that programs are important and that the church benefits from good sound and lighting? Of course I do. I hold crusades in stadiums. Without such tools, a crusade couldn't impact the city we're trying to reach. Likewise, a church couldn't adequately minister to the needs of its community. But when we begin to believe that these supplemental tools are what changes lives, we couldn't be farther from the truth of the Gospel. First and foremost, we need God's power. We need his miracles. Regardless of who they are, people need God's healing. Air conditioning, sound, lighting, comfortable seats, and big screens cannot bring God's healing or transformational power to anyone. If that were the case, hospitals would be replaced with movie theaters. There is no substitute for the power of God, and Christians in Asia, Latin America, and Africa believe that truth with every fiber of their being. Unless we regain a teachable spirit that is guided by humility, we will forever be stuck with spiritual bad breath.

Please hear my heart when I say that if there is anyone who struggles with pride, it's me. Many times, we see in others the thing that we despise in ourselves, and that doesn't sit well. Indeed, I recognize that I have a long way to go to eliminate the pride that keeps me from dying to myself. My desire is to remove the barriers in my life that prevent me from experiencing God's miracle-working power. Why is this so important? Why should God's miracles play such an important part in the life of the believer? Here are several important reasons:

First, without God's miracles, there is no hope for humanity. Without salvation, there is no hope for eternal life. Without deliverance, there is no hope for being set free from the vices of the enemy. Without divine healing, there is no hope for those who are terminally ill, those to whom doctors have said, "Sorry, there is nothing we can do for you." Without God's miracles, what convinces society that God is real or that he interacts with his creation? Without the power of God, what distinguishes Christianity from all the other religions that claim to be the truth?

The miracles in the New Testament marked the difference between Jesus and every other prophet, philosopher, and self-proclaimed spiritual leader. When miracles happen today, they show the world that the Kingdom of God has come and that Christ is backing those who truly believe. Miracles set Jesus apart from other so-called messiahs. They gave him legitimacy. Today, miracles do the same for the body of Christ. Just about every religion can point to miracles that happened thousands of years ago. Only Christianity can say that Jesus continues to do even greater miracles today. In this sense, miracles give the Lord's followers legitimacy and help them reach into the kingdom of darkness to take back that which the enemy has stolen.

Second, I am reminded to rid myself of pride because the Bible commands it. Notice what the Lord says about humility and pride.

> "You save the humble, but your eyes are on the haughty to bring them low" (2 Sam. 22:28).

> "If my people, who are called by my name, will humble themselves and pray and seek my face and turn from their wicked ways, then will I hear from heaven and will forgive their sin and will heal their land" (2 Chron. 7:14).

> "When pride comes, then comes disgrace, but with humility comes wisdom" (Prov. 11:2).

> "Pride only breeds quarrels, but wisdom is found in those who take advice" (Prov. 13:10).

> "A man's pride brings him low, but a man of lowly spirit gains honor" (Prov. 29:23).

In places where miracles occur frequently, followers of Christ take these verses to heart. They understand that the Lord opposes the proud but exalts the humble. Their worship services are different. They generally don't complain about the sound volume, style of music, or how hot or cold it is. Nor are they impressed with sophisticated lighting, big screens, or whether the soloist hits the note at the crescendo. Instead of getting caught up in quarrels, they focus on the reason they came to worship the Lord in the first place. They understand that in the Kingdom of God, their role is to be the best servant they can be. That's a gold nugget! They realize that worship isn't about them or their desires. Instead, they humble themselves and surrender their agenda to the Lordship of Christ.

The True Meaning of Humility

People may or may not believe what we say, but they always believe what we do. People can pretend to be humble with their words, but their actions always give them away. A few years ago, I watched a three-part series on the History Channel produced by the BBC called "Jesus: The Complete Story." It was a historical piece aimed at describing the culture during the times of Christ in the area of Judea.

The third program highlighted how archeologists discovered pathways that were used exclusively by the Pharisees and members of the religious council so they could walk to and from the temple without having to mingle with people in the streets. Many times, these pathways were built over rooftops and through private corridors so that religious leaders could be shielded from people who were considered unclean. As someone in ministry, I find this troubling. Why in the world would the religious leaders of the day want to separate themselves from those who needed God the most? The answer was simple—pride.

As you can imagine, the lifestyle of the religious community infuriated Jesus. This is why he said, "You hypocrites! Isaiah was right when he prophesied about you: 'These people honor me with their lips but their hearts are far from me'" (Matt. 15:7–8). Or, "You brood of vipers, how can you who are evil say anything good? For out of the overflow of the heart the mouth speaks" (Matt. 12:34). Jesus was upset with the religious leaders because they enjoyed all the perks and public recognition of a life of service without truly helping others. Their pride and arrogance prevented them from seeing the true gift of God—Christ, the Messiah—for the people of Israel. That is precisely why there is no record of any Pharisee experiencing a miracle.

Being humble means that we think less about our perks, advancements, or status. It means that we're less concerned about our legacy and accomplishments than we are about those who are hurting and desperately in need of a savior. Again, I am not saying that we shouldn't celebrate accomplishments or legacies. I am simply saying that genuine humility puts the perks and recognition at the bottom of the list of priorities. C. S. Lewis gave us a great definition of humility: "True humility is not thinking less of yourself; it is thinking of yourself less."[1] Someone who thinks about himself or herself less is closer to true servanthood, and servants are greater candidates for God's favor and miracles.

Let's look again at the story in Mark 5:21–43 that exemplifies God's appreciation for those who cast aside their pride and humble themselves. As we discovered in chapter 3, Jairus was a ruler who was a lay official in charge of the management of the synagogue. He probably was familiar with Christ's reputation, and thus, sought his help with a personal need. Jairus fell at Jesus' feet and humbly begged him, "My little daughter is dying. Please come and put your hands on her so that she will be healed and live." Jesus agreed to go with him. All of a sudden the story takes a detour. The woman with the issue of hemorrhaging for twelve years interrupts and detains Jesus for an unspecified amount of time. This delay turns out to be catastrophic for Jairus' daughter. A group of people came from the ruler's home to inform him that the girl had died and that the Messiah's help is no longer necessary.

Jesus recognizes Jairus' faith and humility and ignores the report. He turns to Jairus and says, "Don't be afraid; just believe." His words are a motivation for intense faith.

As Jesus and his three closest disciples approach the house, Jesus finds the funeral has already begun with professional mourners and people crying and wailing loudly. Even a poor man by law would have paid for at least two flute players and one professional mourner. For someone of Jairus' stature, it would have been expected that they would have hired a large number of professional mourners.[1]

Jesus walks into Jairus' house and says, "Why all this commotion and wailing? The child is not dead but asleep." Jesus makes an important point. The girl, whether dead or not, has not been delivered over to the realm of death. She will soon come back. The mourners disagree. They feel she is gone. Their mourning immediately turns into laughter and mocking, which shows how disingenuous and hypocritical they were.

Jesus doesn't respond well to hypocrisy and forces all of them out of the house. He takes the child's father and mother with the three disciples into the child's room. Taking her by the hand, he said to her, *"Talitha koum!"*, which means, "Little girl, I say to you, get up!" Springing out of bed, the little girl begins to walk around without any hindrances. The mother, father, and disciples truly believed the girl had been dead. If they had thought she was asleep, they wouldn't have been amazed by the miracle. Then Jesus gave them strict orders not to tell anyone what happened and instructed them to give the girl something to eat.

The phrase *synagogue ruler* appears four times in the story. Mark obviously was impressed with Jairus' position in the community. In spite of his exalted status, Jairus threw himself at the feet of Jesus and begged him to go and lay his hand on his daughter. Not only does the story show desperation, it depicts humility. It shows that Jairus recognized his position in relationship to Christ's. Think about all the high-level officials you know, regardless of the country in which they live. How many of them who have deathly ill family members have thrown themselves on the ground in a public place or a church and begged Jesus for healing? That is precisely what separates Jairus' humility from others.

Breaking the Pattern of Pride and Arrogance

Whether you feel there are areas in your life that need change or you are leading others who need to push aside their pride, the following thoughts will help you become more like those who experience the power of God in miraculous ways.

Although it was unfortunate that Jairus' daughter was deathly ill, at least he quickly learned there were no other options than to petition Jesus to heal her. He was forced to strip himself of his personal and occupational pride and arrogance. That's what desperation does. If you or those you lead are desperate, you are one step closer to understanding this principle. If not, first *ask God to show you the areas where pride has clouded your vision*. Maybe your status, career, salary, or personal attitudes are preventing you from seeing things clearly.

Second, *ask God to help you see yourself the way he sees you*. Too many people do not see themselves or reality for that matter accurately. They start their day by getting out of the shower, getting dressed, and putting on a false perception. They wear mental glasses that tint the world a different color. They see their friends differently than others. Even worse, though, they do not see themselves accurately. They spend more money than they realize. They eat more food than they should. They gossip more often than they acknowledge. They talk more than they think they do. And at the same time, they justify it. While they might not admit it openly, deep down inside they have a sense of self-righteousness and justification.

This is why it is crucial for every one of us to have a breakthrough in our perception, that is, the way we see ourselves. We must ask God for an accurate paradigm, one that allows us to see ourselves the way he sees us.

Third, *ask God to help you "be transformed by the renewing of your mind"* (Rom. 12:2). Of all the important transformations in life, having a renewed mind is one of the most important. A renewed mind helps you filter out all the competing ideas in your head. A renewed mind cuts down on all the internal struggles and conflicts you frequently feel. A renewed mind gives you the ability to hear God's voice, understand his will, and see his direction. Notice what Paul writes in the second sentence of that Bible verse, "Then you will be able to test and approve what God's will is—his good, pleasing and perfect will." Many people have no idea what the will of God is. Why? Their mind has never been renewed. They've never been transformed.

So how does transformation happen? Paul states the process in the verse before. "Therefore, I urge you, brothers, in view of God's mercy, to offer your bodies as living sacrifices, holy and pleasing to God—this is your spiritual act of worship" (Rom. 12:1). Only humble people can truly offer themselves as living sacrifices in spiritual worship. You cannot fake it or reproduce it. The only way is to humbly offer yourself to God.

Once you've given up everything and offered yourself to him, your mind will be transformed and renewed. Then you will be able to embrace God's paradigm for your life.

Friend, it's imperative that you humble yourself before the Lord. Perhaps you need to reboot your life. Maybe you need to be transformed by the renewing of your mind. If you struggle with arrogance and stubborn pride that blinds you from the way things truly are, now more than ever you need the power of God to transform your life. With pride out of the way, you will be able to see God's good and pleasing will. Then, you will *become what you believe!*

I want to offer you the following prayer, because I believe that God answers when we call upon his name. I want to encourage you to find a place where you can be alone without any distractions. Clear your mind from all the stress and to-do lists, and pray this simple prayer with me. The only thing God asks of you is to pray with a sincere heart.

Father, I ask that you would allow the scales over my eyes to drop so that I can see my life as you see it. Help my confidence to be based upon what you think of me. Help my self-image to reflect a child of God. I realize that pride is a wall of protection. Show me the areas of pride that are keeping me from experiencing your miracle-working power. I ask you for a breakthrough, and I don't want my stubborn arrogance to stand in the way.

I ask you to show me the areas where pride has clouded my vision. Whether my status, salary, or personal attitudes stand in the way, give me the mind of Christ. I offer my life to you as a living sacrifice. Please take it. Transform me and renew my mind. In Christ's name, I pray. Amen.

Questions for discussion or personal reflection

1. In what ways do you struggle with pride?

2. In what ways would your spouse, best friend, or family members say that you struggle with pride?

3. In what ways are you arrogant and unteachable?

4. How has your stubbornness prevented your spiritual growth?

5. What are some ways you can become more teachable?

Chapter Ten
AGENTS OF CHANGE

When my friend David invited me to share in the youth convention in Central America, I thought it would be similar to their annual activity with young people excited to reconnect their lives with God, hear a challenging word, and spend time in dynamic worship. I was only partially correct. To them, the conference was an event to equip and launch their young people to be agents of change. Within weeks of my invitation, their team had produced several videos that were floating around the Internet about how God calls us to be New Testament disciples. The videos showed suffering people in the streets of Central America, many of them homeless and caught in the clutches of drugs. After showing the desperation of countless people, the videos ended with the same phrase: "I will not keep quiet. God has called me to be an agent of change."

As the convention neared, thousands of young people had seen the videos. They were anticipating something revolutionary. That night after the service, the altar was packed to capacity. This time, it wasn't to receive healing or a miracle. They came forward to receive power to go and fulfill what God called them to do. They wanted to see the same miracles the disciples saw when they walked with Jesus, and they wanted to use those miracles to bring people to Christ.

The altar call lasted over an hour. The leadership and I prayed for every single young person in the arena. When we were finished, I received a powerful insight into how Latin Americans view God's power. It's true that people ask for prayer regarding a specific need in almost every country. However, in those areas where miracles are frequent, people are also likely to ask for power to become agents of spreading the Good News to others who need it as well. After all, if God can heal them, he can heal their uncle, friend, or coworker. And God can use them to perform the miracle.

In the United States and Western Europe, we do not necessarily see ourselves as having the same power that Jesus gave the disciples when he sent them out to cast out demons, heal the sick, and proclaim the Good News (Matt. 10:1, Mark 6:7, Luke 9:1, Luke 10:9). Asian, Latin American, and African believers, in contrast, believe they do!

The tenth characteristic found in those who experience the miraculous is the *conviction that they are agents of change*. They believe that they can receive God's miracles and then with the power of God take that message of hope to everyone else who needs it. They truly believe they are connected to the first-century church and that the only thing that separates them from the day of Pentecost is time.

The Direct Connection

One of the reasons people in other parts of the world have New Testament faith is that they believe that Jesus is the same yesterday, today, and forever (Heb. 13:8). They believe that the charge he gave his disciples two thousand years ago is the same charge you and I have today. Nothing has changed. They take to heart the following verses: "And these signs will accompany those who believe: In my name they will drive out demons; they will speak in new tongues" (Mark 16:17). And, "Then the disciples went out and preached everywhere, and the Lord worked with them and confirmed his word by the signs that accompanied it" (Mark 16:20).

The context of both of these scripture verses lies at the heart of the Great Commission. So people with New Testament faith wholeheartedly believe that the purpose behind miracles, signs, and wonders is not to have a spiritual private party for members only. Instead, they believe God performs healings and miracles through them to demonstrate that he is real and that he interacts with his creation. This is what Jesus taught his disciples two thousand years ago.

Jesus called his twelve disciples to him and "gave them authority to drive out evil spirits and to heal every disease and sickness." Then he sent them out with the following instructions, "Go rather to the lost sheep of Israel. As you go, preach this message: 'The kingdom of heaven is near.' Heal the sick, raise the dead, cleanse those who have leprosy, drive out demons. Freely you have received, freely give" (Matt. 10:6–8).

Our friends around the world read these scriptures and believe their call is to do the same, to continue the mission that the disciples started. They can freely receive and freely give. They see themselves as vessels of God's power—as recipients and distributors. There is no separation between being a recipient of something miraculous and the evangelistic call to take that power to other people who need it.

We North Americans and Western Europeans tend to fragment our lives and compartmentalize our roles. We maintain a separation between being receivers of a personal miracle and taking that power to others. Either we freely receive, or we freely give, but combining the two isn't easy for us. There are people who do nothing but receive, and there's a smaller group that simply gives. A New Testament disciple does both.

There Are No Benchwarmers

Why is receiving and giving so important? It keeps us balanced between being an eyewitness to God's power and being someone who proclaims it. Being people who can freely receive God's miracle helps us be powerful eyewitnesses to those who have yet to receive. We can testify to the legitimacy of God's interactive work. But if we simply sit back and receive, eventually our lives grow stale. If all we do is give and never receive, then the quality of what we have to offer becomes dry, routine, and ultimately ineffective. For that reason, the Christian workers in Africa, Asia, and Latin America are numerous. As soon as someone gives his or her life to Christ, they are discipled and put to work. Everyone has a call. Everyone is a disciple. Everyone expects to produce fruit. There are no benchwarmers.

Our home church in Moravia, Costa Rica, has about ten thousand members. It started in a small dirt lot with a tin roof that covered the stage. Richard Jeffrey began the work in 1975 using a Pentecostal evangelistic approach tied directly to divine healing and miracles. From 1975 to 1987 the church grew from 0 to 2,500. Between the cell groups and outstations started, the church influenced more than twenty-four thousand people. From 1987 to 1996 the church grew to well over seven thousand, with outstation and cell group influence numbering more than forty thousand. My family and I joined the church in 1991. Today, they have planted over twenty strong churches throughout the country, many of them with worshippers numbering in the thousands.

This church evangelizes new believers, trains them, and sends them out to win more people with the power of God. People are taught from the beginning that everyone is a disciple and is called to reach those who need God's love. They freely receive and freely give. They view themselves as an open vessel, one that allows God's goodness and power to flow through them.

The Bible talks about this concept in 2 Kings 4:1–7. During the time of the account, there was a terrible drought. The economy was in shambles. People could hardly make ends meet. To make matters worse, a creditor came to a widow demanding that her late husband's debt be paid. "If you don't pay the debt, I will take your two sons to be my slaves," the creditor told the woman. The distraught woman cried out to Elisha and told him everything. "Your servant my husband is dead," she said. "He revered the Lord, but now his creditor is coming to take my two boys as his slaves" (v. 1).

Elisha replied, "How can I help you? Tell me, what do you have in your house?" (v. 2). "I have nothing in my home at all," she replied, "except a little oil." Elisha said, "Take your sons and go to all your neighbors and ask them to give you empty jars. Don't just ask for a couple. Get as many as you can. Then go back to your home, go inside, and shut the door behind you and your boys. Take your oil and begin to fill each jar. As one jar fills up, put it to one side, and start filling the next one" (vv. 3–4).

The widow started to pour the oil, and as each jar was filled she placed it to one side, and her boys handed her another one. She kept pouring until finally, when all the jars were full, she said to her son, "Bring me another jar." "We've filled all the jars we collected," he said. Suddenly, the oil stopped flowing. Then the widow went to Elisha and told him everything that happened and all the oil she had at her disposal. It was worth a decent price. He told her, "Go, sell the oil and pay your debts.

You and your sons can live on what is left" (v. 7).

This story tells me that God provides for those who seek him. It also shows me that while there was a jar to be filled, the oil continued to flow. When there were no more jars, the oil dried up. In the same way, when Christians do not receive power and share it with others, the power dries up. One of the main reasons we are not experiencing revival in the United States and Western Europe is that a vast majority of believers have become receivers and do not pour what God has given them into other people. They do not take the message of the Gospel or the power of God to those who need it.

On a broader scale, we have fewer evangelists now than ever. In the last twenty years, it has become politically incorrect to share our faith. So Christians keep their spiritual opinions to themselves. Contrast that with the believers around the world and those in the book of Acts, and we can see a major difference between them and us.

Moving from the Fringes of God's Will to the Center

One way to begin breaking the cycle is to see ourselves as people through whom God wants to do miracles. It's true. He wants to do miracles through you. He is looking for agents. Few people are willing to take the charge and step out in faith to proclaim that "the Kingdom of God is at hand" (Mark 1:14), "to preach good news to the poor, to proclaim freedom for the prisoners, and recovery of sight for the blind, to release the oppressed, to proclaim the year of the Lord's favor" (Luke 4:18–19). There are few workers, and it's fair to say that per capita, there are fewer workers today than when Jesus founded his church two thousand years ago. So then, decide to be an agent.

Move from the fringe to the center of God's will.

Then step out in faith to demonstrate that God is real and interacts with his creation, all with the motive of seeing people come to a life-changing encounter with Christ. That's the reason behind this book. Signs, wonders, healings, and miracles all exist for the purpose of convincing people that God is real. His power is real. He simply desires to show people that Christ is Lord and that he is the only way to heaven. Miracles are, among other things, the evidence that what God says in his word is true. Without miracles, the Gospel becomes one of many other religious philosophies that people try to explain away. With miracles, people are awakened to the most important and universal truth. A life with God is infinitely greater than a life without him. Christians in Latin America, Asia, and Africa believe this in the core of their being. That is why they live out their Christian convictions to the fullest.

I want to encourage you to become a New Testament believer. Lay aside the apathy, distractions, and hesitations you have and move from the fringes of God's will to the center of it. Become an agent of dynamic change. Lay hands on the sick. Pray for the blind. Bind up the brokenhearted. Proclaim freedom to the prisoners. Break the chains of the oppressed. Proclaim the miracles that God does. Spread the word and encourage others. If you don't, who will? Be the agent God is calling you to be. If the pages of this book have had any impact on you, then in Jesus' name, *become what you believe!*

I want to leave you with this final prayer as a model for submitting yourself to the Lord as his agent. May you sense he is commissioning you to do great and mighty things in Jesus' name. May the Lord empower you to be his agent of change.

Lord, I humbly ask you to empower me to be your agent in a dark world that needs your love. This world needs your powerful touch. We all need an encounter with you. Open the floodgates of heaven and pour out a powerful revival that glorifies your name. Heal the sick. Give sight to the blind. Bind up the brokenhearted. Liberate the oppressed. Use me, Lord, in this Great Commission.

Help me to be your agent of change in the midst of a world that desperately needs you. Fill me and empower me with your Spirit. Help me to see the doors you open to reach others who need your salvation and power. In Christ's name, I pray. Amen.

Questions for discussion or personal reflection

1. Have you noticed that people in your spiritual social circles tend to be receivers or givers? How would you describe the difference between the two? Are there people in your life who have experienced the miraculous but then go on to help others receive miracles as well? How would you describe their walk with the Lord?

2. In what ways do you believe God wants you to become an agent of change?

3. What are some of the things that stand in your way of becoming an agent of change? How can others help you overcome those obstacles?

4. What one type of miracle do you want to see happen before you meet the Lord? How do you want God to use you in the miraculous?

Conclusion

It was a hot August day in 2009. My wife, Cindee, and I were invited to lunch by Dr. Robert H. Schuller, the founding pastor of the Crystal Cathedral. He wanted to meet with me prior to my first speaking engagement on the "Hour of Power" program. We stepped into the partial glass elevator and took in the beautiful view of Orange County as we ascended the thirteen-story office building adjacent to the Cathedral.

As we stepped out, Dr. Schuller's assistant immediately greeted us and said, "Dr. Schuller is ready to see you." I rounded the corner, and there the eighty-two-year-old pastor stood with an outstretched hand ready to greet me. After a few small pleasantries, we took our seats around the large table prepared for lunch. His wife, Arvella, joined us, along with his daughters, Sheila and Gretchen.

Over the course of our two-hour lunch, the Reformed Church of America pastor shared several insightful principles. Then he put down his turkey sandwich, and looked me in the eye as if to say, this is the most important thing I will ever say to you. "Jason," he said, "I've been criticized for not preaching on sin. That's simply not true. Most of my critics who believe that have a superficial definition of sin. Mine is much more profound." I sat back in my chair and thought to myself, "I'd like to hear that definition."

He went on to say, "The greatest sin is the sin of unbelief. After wandering in the desert for forty years, the Israelites did not enter into their rest according to the book of Hebrews because of their unbelief. That is why I've spent my life trying to convince people to believe." He was absolutely right! Unbelief trumps all other sins.

As I mentioned in chapter 2, persecution has not been part of our discussion of miracles. Neither has poverty. While it's true that people who suffer through persecution and poverty tend to be more desperate because they have fewer options, in the New Testament people were not persecuted nor were they caught in the clutches of extreme poverty when Jesus performed his miracles. My concern is that Christians in the United States are not too far behind.

When I asked a few of my colleagues who work in Western Europe why they feel revival has not swept the European continent, they gave me some interesting insights. They felt that Western Europeans have been fooled too many times. They have lost trust in those who have led their religious institutions. Over the centuries, they've been lied to, misguided, and in many ways have been treated like those who were under the Pharisees in the first century. So what we have left are people who are culturally Christian and complete their religious duties dictated to them by a church that hardly believes in miracles itself.

The entire focus of this book has been to capture the commonalities between the recipients of the miraculous in the New Testament and those who experience miracles around the world today. We have studied ten characteristics of those who experience the miraculous.

First, those who received a miracle in the New Testament, like those who do today, have a worldview that is much more holistic than ours. They see the natural and supernatural world on the same continuum. They do not fragment or separate the two. To them, these two worlds are intertwined and impact the other. The Kingdom of God and the kingdom of darkness impact the material world, and the decisions we make as human beings have significant consequences in the supernatural world.

Second, people who experience miracles have a strong sense of urgency and desperation. They do not have the luxury of depending on an insurance company, hospital, or social security to take care of their needs. For them, they have one option—God. Unless he comes through for them, there is no hope. In contrast, Western Europeans and North Americans have a plethora of options. We have systems in place that create a firewall of protection to keep us from suffering, pain, and inconvenience. While these systems are wonderful, they reduce the role God plays in our life. He becomes one additional option we may or may not turn to in our time of need.

Third, people who experience the miraculous tend to be convinced that Christ is their solution even before their encounter with him. They have heard about Christ's power through testimonies. They heard the stories of other people who were healed or who experienced his power. When they are told that Jesus can do the same in their life, they believe. Many of us who were raised in areas where having faith is seen as parochial or gullible tend to discount miracle stories. We look for a logical explanation and lean heavily on scientific verification before we commit to a *miraculous* conclusion.

Fourth, miracles occur when people have profound respect and honor for spiritual authority. These people treat those in ministry with respect, but most importantly, they realize where they are in the spiritual pecking order. They not only submit to authority, they teach their children how to do the same. How else can a parent demand respect from her child if she doesn't model respect for that child? We learn to how to show honor and respect by seeing a healthy example in others. Insubordination isn't tolerated in the armed forces, so why would we think that the Lord would allow it in the Kingdom of God? In contrast, over the last 250 years Western Europe and North America have been at the center of countless regional, civil, and world wars. Now more then ever, there is an attitude of pessimism and contempt for those in government leadership. The struggle between rebelliousness and submission is rooted deep in the Western mindset and inevitably spills over into our church life. Learning to push our stubbornness to one side will ultimately create a deep respect for God's authority and set a foundation for true humility.

Fifth, people who experience miracles have no problem believing that miracles can happen through a process and over time. North Americans and Western Europeans are very conscious of time. As a matter of fact, they do everything they can to preserve it and not waste it. If we try a remedy and nothing happens, we move on to another solution. Believers in Latin America, Africa, and Asia view time differently than we do. That is why church events, weddings, and family reunions in these regions can last hours, days, or longer. Miracles can take days, months, or even years. If you ask them when God's hand moved, they don't pinpoint a specific time. They think in terms of process.

Sixth, Christians in Asia, Africa, and Latin America have a slightly different definition of the term *belief* than we do. When they believe in something, their belief doesn't stay confined within the walls of a theoretical or philosophical idea. Instead, their beliefs move to convictions. That makes them willing to take action and publicly verbalize their faith in the Lord before the miracle occurs. Further, even in those cases when the evidence was contrary, just like those in the New Testament (the woman in Matt 15:28, the royal official in John 4:50, Jairus in

Luke 8:50, the ten lepers in Luke 17:14, the centurion in Luke 7:10), they believe the Lord when he tells them their miracle is coming.

Seventh, people in different parts of the world who frequently experience miracles have a spirit of bravado and display a willingness to break social norms in order to get to the source of their miracle. Much like the woman with the issue of blood in Mark 5, people who have no options are willing to go to great lengths to get what they need. They will aggressively push to the front of the line in order to reach out and touch the hem of the Lord's garment. In contrast, people who live in developed countries have a plethora of options and tend to be more reluctant to *embarrass* themselves by breaking social rules in order to receive their remedy.

Eighth, the suppliants are persistent even when it seems that God ignores them. In many ways, they are not willing to take no for an answer. Like the widow dealing with the unjust judge (Luke 18:5) or the mother whose daughter was tormented by demon possession (Matt. 15:27), our friends overseas have an uncanny ability to pursue God's favor even when he is silent. When most of us who live in the United States and parts of Western Europe take God's silence as a negative, they see it for what it is, a test of faith.

Ninth, those in the New Testament along with our brothers and sisters in other parts of the world who see the miraculous tend not to think of themselves too highly. Nor do they believe that their accomplishments are extraordinary or that they possess any special gift. Instead, they genuinely and humbly seek the Lord, because they know that God always opposes the proud. Because of their humility, they are easier to guide, teach, and lead.

Tenth, those who experience miracles see themselves as agents of spreading the Good News and demonstrating God's power to as many people as they can. Miracles are not just for their benefit. Just like the gift of salvation, God's power is for everyone who needs it. They realize that God never gives us a gift without expecting us to use it. People who want to experience miracles without the desire to use them to touch other people's lives are not worthy of receiving miracles. That is why Jesus empowered his disciples and sent them out.

With these ten areas in mind, I want to encourage you to go out just as the disciples did. Pray for others. Believe that God will use you to demonstrate to an incredulous world that indeed he exists and still does the miraculous. If you've become convinced through these pages that God desires to perform miracles in your life, ask him to use you and open doors. There is no magical formula or special technique. All you need is a genuine heart and faith. God will do the rest.

Finally, I want to leave you with several things you can do to turn the tide in your personal life. Look for ways to spend time with Hispanic, Asian, and African Christians. Look for first-generation believers who have immigrated into your area. Become their friends, and try to see the world from their perspective.

Spend time reaching out to those who are poor. Remember, Jesus said, "When you've done it to the least of these my brethren, you've done it unto me." Become involved in compassion ministries, remembering that the motivation is not doing it *for* Jesus but *to* Jesus. Otherwise, we risk making it a social gospel. You are not helping Jesus when you help them. Instead, try reaching out to them as if you were helping Jesus himself.

Finally, go overseas on a mission trip as often as you can.

Learn from the pastors and spiritual leaders who live in those areas where miracles are more frequent. Listen to the testimonies the people give when God does something miraculous in their lives. Ask them to pray for you and impart the revival into you. Even more important, discover how they view the supernatural world and perceive its impact on the material world. Then continue your relationship with them through e-mail, social media, or videoconferencing.

If I could summarize this entire book in a phrase, I would say that people experience the miraculous because they take the Lord at his word. They believe him in spite of the headwinds, setbacks, and discouraging news. They believe him regardless of professional diagnosis, secular philosophies and contrarian societal ideas. They choose to believe. Inevitably, they *do* become what they believe. So, friend, take God at his word. Believe him when he says that he gives you power to do greater things in his name than what the disciples did two thousand years ago. If you *really* believe God can do it, then **BECOME WHAT YOU BELIEVE!**

ACKNOWLEDGMENTS

Thank you, Dick and Jan for your wonderful mentorship over the years. I am far less than a weak shadow of Moses, but you are definitely a Jethrow. You two are some of the finest people I know, and all who know you have been greatly enriched by your love and faith! On behalf of the millions of people in Latin America that have been touched by your efforts, thank you!

Thank you, Cindee, Celina, Chanel, and Jazmin for patiently waiting for me to finish this important work. Through thick and thin, you've stood by me, believed in me, and loved me unconditionally. I am proud and so honored to call you my wife and daughters.

Thank you, Kathleen Stevens for diligently working to edit this book and make it what it is. You helped it become what I believed it would become. You have such a gift as an editor, and you are a pure joy to work with.

Thank you, Rick Cortez for creating a fabulous cover. Few people have your talents and gifts to create such beauty. Thanks for your friendship over the years and for being a wonderful Christian to my family and me.

Thank you, John Salmon for translating this document into the heavenly language. Your dedication to professionalism is highly evident, and you are one of the finest in the art of linguistic contextualization.

Thank you, Joe Class for the insightful conversations that sparked the first chapter of this book. God has used you powerfully and given you a brilliantly creative mind to see the invisible.

Thank you, Carlos Annacondia for sharing your precious

story of the man from Mar Del Plata with me and every reader that picks up this book. You have impacted my life in such a profound way. Millions of people's lives have been transformed through the words that the Spirit of God has spoken through you.

Thank you, Don and Melba Exley for your powerful insights into the revival in Argentina. Some of the most meaningful spiritual times have been when the Lord used you to deeply impact my life. I love and appreciate you both!

Thank you, all my friends at the Ziglar Corporation for your outstanding and unwavering support over the years. You exemplify what it means to live a Christian life in a world that is becoming increasingly secular.

Thank you, David Godwin, Raúl Vargas, Dave Ellis, Dick Nicholson, Mari-Lee Ruddy, Cindy Riggins, Levoy Dewey, Cindy Larson, Steve Harrison, Bill Harrison, and everyone else who poured over the pages of this work and gave helpful feedback.

Endnotes

Introduction

1. See http://www.barna.org/faith-spirituality/514-barna-study-of-religious-change-since-1991-shows-significant-changes-by-faith-group
2. Zig Ziglar, Zig Ziglar's Little Book of Big Quotes (Plano, TX: Ziglar, Inc., 2008).
3. Craig S. Keener, Miracles: The Credibility of the New Testament Accounts (Grand Rapids, MI: Baker Publishing Group), Kindle edition.

Chapter One

1. Jason Frenn, Breaking the Barriers: Overcoming Adversity and Reaching Your Greatest Potential (Nashville: Faith-Words, 2009).

Chapter Two

1. See http://neo.jpl.nasa.gov/news/fireball_130301.html
2. See http://www.cnn.com/2013/02/15/travel/triumph-cruise-crew
3. Jason Frenn, Power to Reinvent Yourself: How to Break the Destructive Patterns in Your Life (Nashville: Faith-Words, 2010).

Chapter Three

1. James Strong, Strong's Greek Dictionary of the Bible (Mik

lal Software Solutions, 2011), Kindle edition, Kindle location 48357.
2. See Bible Hub, http://biblesuite.com/greek/4487.htm

Chapter Four

1. Zig Ziglar, Zig Ziglar's Little Book of Big Quotes (Plano, TX: Ziglar, Inc., 2008).

Chapter Six

1. R. T. France, The Gospel of Matthew (New International Commentary on the New Testament) (Grand Rapids, MI: Wm. B. Eerdmans Publishing Co., 2007), Kindle edition, 368.
2. Craig S. Keener, Miracles.
3. The Pentecostal Evangel, www.pe.ag.org

Chapter Seven

1. Joel B. Green, The Gospel of Luke (The New International Commentary on the New Testament) (Grand Rapids, MI: Wm. B. Eerdmans Publishing Co.), Kindle edition, 641.
2. Joel B. Green, The Gospel of Luke, 237.

Chapter Eight

1. R. T. France, The Gospel of Matthew, 595.

Chapter Nine

1. C. S. Lewis, Mere Christianity (San Francisco: Harper San Francisco, 2009).
2. William L. Lane, The Gospel According to Mark: The En glish Text with Introduction, Exposition, and Notes (The New International Commentary on the New Testament) (Grand Rapids, MI: Wm. B. Eerdmans Publishing Co., 1974), Kindle Edition, Kindle location 2071.

Dear friend,

I am pleased that you picked up this book and started to read some of the life-changing things that God has been orchestrating in meetings all around the world. May you experience God's mighty hand in your life and in the ones you love.

I pray you'll be inspired, encouraged, and motivated to join with us to reach 100 million people who need God's help. We are dependent upon God to be a ministry that effectively communicates the Gospel to everyone who has not made a commitment to Christ by utilizing public evangelistic meetings, radio, television, writing, & Internet. You can join with us in prayer, monthly support, or volunteering in an outreach.

Connect with us through any of the following ways:

www.frenn.org
www.JasonFrenn.com
twitter.com/jasonfrenn
Facebook.com/jasonfrenn
Youtube.com/jasonfrenn

May the Lord continue to bless you richly!

Jason Frenn

© Photo by John Ehde

Notes and Reflection

Notes and Reflection